The
444
Connection

J. K. Womelsdorf

ISBN-10: 0984944427
ISBN-13: 978-0984944422

DEDICATION

To my Grandfather, whom I never knew; and also to my friend Jeff, without whose help this book would not have been possible.

CONTENTS

FORWARD

It has taken me over ten years to come to terms with the spiritual experience that I went through for many years. And although it seems as if this spiritual experience is now over for me, I am beginning to realize that it will never really be over for any of us. We are all in this world together, experiencing different things, and at different times. The spiritual experience that I am speaking about was really an accelerated spiritual experience that left me worn, but alive; alive with volumes of spiritual information that may only make sense to me, but could possibly help others in their search for greater meaning in this life. My search has just begun, really, but I am currently sifting through all of the spiritual information and memories that I have retained from the spiritual crisis that I went through.

   In the pages that follow are vignettes of the highlights of my experience, both good and bad, that were about things that I experienced and things that I learned, that have shaped my current spiritual beliefs. It was very difficult, at first, for me to revisit this time in my life because of the very deep challenges that I had to face in order to arrive at a more peaceful point in my life. I pray to God every day now and many of my prayers include many heartfelt thanks to God for His mercy and the peace that He has graced my life with now.

It is interesting to me that I went through such a difficult time and yet never stopped smiling at people I knew. I often wonder if there are people that I know in my life now who may be suffering a similar crisis and yet are smiling throughout their days, as well; with their spiritual crisis remaining unknown to others that they may know. If the information in this book could help even one person in this world today, then that would make my very dark spiritual experience that I went through, a little lighter. And while it has taken me many years to understand this, it was my spiritual journey, or experience, that ultimately won me over to God and His love for me.

I realize that there may be inconsistencies and possibly even contradictions in the messages of this book. But spirituality itself can be a very hard thing to describe. I experienced incredibly different things throughout my spiritual experience and believed that each experience that I went through was the truth. In the end, I was left to try and explain to myself and others what had happened to me, as well as what I had learned from my experience. This book is the result of my efforts to relate just what it was that I went through and learned. There are many other things that I could have written about, but I stuck with those things that left the deepest impression upon me.

PART ONE

THE 444 CONNECTION

THE NUMBER 444

444 a.m.; I stared at my digital clock for what seemed to be a very long time. It seemed longer than a minute, but yet there it was, the number 444. I thought to myself, how strange this was, almost as if this number meant something. This was the first time I had woken up at this time of the morning that I could ever remember. I was a little disturbed because I had set my alarm clock for 6:30 a.m., yet I could not get back to sleep.

It was September of 1991 and I was working in Atlanta, Georgia for a major airline as a flight attendant. Every year we were required as flight attendants to attend a one day safety training course. On this particular day I was scheduled to attend my annual flight attendant training course and was looking forward to getting a good night's sleep.

However, I kept thinking about how I had awoken at 444 a.m. and I couldn't seem to get back to sleep. Staring at this number for what seemed like an eternity had given me a strange feeling that I had not felt before. I felt like this number meant something, but I had no idea what. I remember it was kind of an eerie feeling, almost as if something was trying to grab my attention. But what could it be...?

Later that morning as I was driving to my annual flight attendant training class, the thought of this number slowly left my mind. I had basically forgotten about waking up at 444 a.m. that morning. When I finally arrived at my training site and had taken my seat in the classroom, I began to wonder what the topics would be for our safety training class. My instructor soon entered the room and began our safety training. Everything was pretty much as I expected it would be until later in the day when our instructor told us about why we should always be prepared for safety on an airplane. He was talking about what we should do as flight attendants if something were to go wrong while we were working on a flight. At one point he talked about an actual plane that had crashed and mentioned that the number of the flight was 444. I couldn't believe it. There was that number again, twice in one day! I remember thinking how strange this was and how it seemed like it was more than just coincidence.

A few days passed by and I finally told a few friends about what had happened. I explained to them that I had woken up at 444 a.m. and was staring at this number on my digital clock. I then explained what had happened when I was at my annual training and how my instructor had mentioned this number again. Since they were my friends they didn't think I was crazy, but I could tell that they didn't understand what I was feeling about this strange occurrence. They seemed to be more impressed about the story of the plane crash that I had related to them than the actual sighting of the number 444 several times in one day.

However, this changed quickly. One of my friends, who was also a flight attendant for the same airline I worked for, was called to work the next day by our scheduling department. At the airline I worked at, every trip that a flight attendant was assigned had a trip number that went with it. When my friend heard that her trip number was going to be 444, she couldn't believe it. She accepted the assignment from the airline's scheduling department and immediately called our other friend, since I was working that day and was unavailable for a phone call from her. Apparently, my friend was very scared about this number since it had been associated with a plane crash. She didn't know what to do. Ultimately she went to work and everything was fine.

When she eventually told me what had happened, I

couldn't believe it. She thought maybe I had played a trick on her until I reminded her that I had seen this number before she had been assigned the trip number 444. We both knew that something was going on with this number, but we didn't know what it was or what it meant. This left a big impression on me and I kept thinking about this number for the next couple of days. The whole event carried with it a very deep feeling and I knew that somehow I was being influenced by something that was much greater than I could understand.

There were many feelings that I began to associate with this number and for the most part I had trouble figuring them out. There were feelings of astonishment, wonder and even some fearful feelings. This had never happened to me before, although I was no stranger to odd events happening to me in my life. Throughout my life I had always been able to see things that were going to happen to me in the near future. They were mostly mundane things though. For example, many times before a song was played on the radio, I knew which song was going to be played a few seconds before it came on the radio. This would happen every so often. Another example of this was when I knew the phone was going to ring a few seconds before it actually did. This too would happen from time to time. I didn't think much about these things because most people I talked to about them either didn't believe me or didn't care much about them.

But this time it was different. I had actually told a friend about what had happened to me with the number 444 and then something had happened to her the next day with the number 444. This was unbelievably strange. This solidified a certain belief in me that this number meant something. Although as to what it might mean, I had no idea.

It seemed like the next time I saw this number was a couple of weeks later. During this time I thought about what had happened to me occasionally but I was not as impressed by it as I had been on the day that I had seen this number twice. However, when I did see the number 444 again it was very impressive because of the way that it happened and because of the feeling that it would leave me with.

It happened one evening when I walked into my apartment in Atlanta and turned on the television. The weekly lottery pick was on the television and the number 444 was the winning number. There it was again! I thought it was very strange that this number was on the television exactly when I turned it on. There was the same unexplained feeling that I had received when I first saw this number. I did begin to wonder though if this was pure coincidence. But the 444 sightings continued in ways that became even more astounding to me. One time in particular was very strange to me and it kind of pushed me over the edge as far as wondering if this was pure coincidence.

It happened one day when I was at work as a flight attendant at an airport. I was helping the ticket agents board the passengers onto the plane that I was going to be working on. We had to greet the passengers who were boarding the plane and then take their ticket and let them proceed onto the plane. I was always very careful to look at the passenger's tickets when I was taking them to make sure that they were boarding the correct flight. I was sure that the ticket agents who were helping me were being just as careful.

But about halfway through the boarding process, a passenger who had boarded the plane walked back up the jet way, from the plane, and handed me her ticket stub. She had apparently boarded the airplane but had discovered that she was on the wrong flight. So I took her ticket stub from her to try and figure out what had happened. When I looked at it I couldn't believe what I saw. She was supposed to be on a different flight that had a flight number of 444. She was also supposed to be flying on an entirely different airline than the one I was working for. How could this have happened? I didn't know what was stranger- the fact that she had been allowed to board our plane when she was supposed to be on another airline with a different flight number, or that I was staring at the number 444 again!

We helped this woman get to her correct flight and then we prepared for takeoff on the flight that I was working on. What happened next only added to the very odd feeling I felt about seeing the number 444 again. When the plane that I was working on had been fully boarded, it pushed back from the gate and prepared for takeoff. Soon after takeoff, there was a flock of birds that our plane ended up flying through. Unfortunately, a few of the birds went through one of our engines and this created a fire in that engine. The pilots were able to extinguish this fire quickly with the automatic engine fire extinguisher system and they turned the plane around and landed safely. This was a very scary event that I had just gone through and I knew that things could have been much worse.

When we came back to the airport and deplaned, I remember thinking about how odd it was that I had just seen the number 444 before all this had happened. I couldn't figure it out. Was this a good thing or a bad thing. I thought maybe this number was causing bad things to happen to me. It seemed to be much more than a coincidence that I had seen this number before our plane lost an engine during takeoff. But then I thought maybe this number was a sign that I was going to be all right. Even though I had just gone through a very scary event, the outcome was very positive. After all, we landed safely and we all deplaned without any injuries.

This thought would haunt me through the years when I continued to see this number. Was this number a sign of bad things to come? Or was it a sign that I was being helped by an unknown force? Sometimes I felt an unexplained sense of doom, whenever I saw this number, and this did not help my opinion of what was happening to me. It was almost like I was thinking, "Oh no, there's that number again. What's going to happen next?"

The sightings continued. I call them sightings because it became a very strange phenomenon to me. I was no longer only seeing this number in very strange ways, but I was going through some very bizarre events that I began to associate with this number. There were many instances when I saw this number on the license plate of a car, just when I had been thinking about this number. And the way in which some cars that had this number on their license plate would cut me off in traffic, when I was driving, was ridiculous. The cars seemed to cut me off when I was driving and then slow down so that the number 444 on the license plate would be right in front of me. It was almost unbelievable. Most of the time this number would be just a part of the whole license plate number. Although one time I saw just the number 444 on a license plate and I began to wonder if the person driving this car had been seeing this number too? Could there be other people besides my friend in Atlanta that had seen the number 444? Because, my friend was the only other person that I knew of that had seen this number too.

The internet was just beginning to arrive in many households around the world during the time I started to see this number. So the thought of checking the internet to see if anyone else was also seeing this number didn't cross my mind at the time. It seemed as if I was going through this experience on my own. There didn't seem to be anyone that I could relate to about these strange occurrences. During this time I was not very religious. I did not go to church, nor did I pray to God or Jesus. Although I had been raised as a child in what most people would call a "different" type of religion that professed healing through faith and spiritual understanding. But this religious upbringing did not stick with me in my life and I had no real anchor to anything relating to God. Although I did believe in God to a certain extent, I did not think that this could be something spiritual that I was going through. Rather, I thought that it was just plain strange; something that could simply not be explained and definitely something that I could not relate to with anyone.

For the next couple of years I saw this number at random intervals and in very interesting ways. Sometimes a couple of weeks would go by until I saw this number and sometimes it seemed like a month or so would go by before I saw it again. But it would continue to appear in my life and it seemed like this number always had some meaning behind it.

In 1995 I moved to a small town in New Hampshire where the intensity of this number seemed to pick up considerably. I still kept waking up occasionally at 4:44 a.m., but other 444 sightings occurred with more meaning to them. At one point when I was remodeling the older house that I was living in, I remember looking around my neighborhood and deciding that it could really use some fixing up itself. But I knew that this was out of my control. Even though the streets had plenty of potholes and the sidewalks had long since crumbled apart, I knew that the town I was living in, was having to stretch the money that it had. It seemed like the streets would have to wait a while before they were improved.

Several weeks later I woke up one morning to the sound of construction going on down the street. I walked out of my house and saw a construction crew tearing up the street in order to get it ready to be repaved. I soon found out that all the streets in my neighborhood were going to be repaved and that new sidewalks were going to be added as well. What a shock! It was the timing that really surprised me. I had just been thinking about this several weeks before. And these streets hadn't been repaved in many, many years. Why now?

The real shock occurred a few weeks later. It was after all the streets had been paved and the construction crew was almost finished. I was sitting on my front porch when a huge piece of construction equipment, that had been used to repave the streets, pulled up right in front of my driveway and stopped. I had not seen this particular piece of equipment before. The driver stepped out and walked down the street to do something else for a while. It was then that I saw the number 444. It was on the side of the big piece of construction equipment. Apparently this was the machine's assigned number and the number 444 was just sitting there as if to say, "This is what you wanted, so this is what you get". I was astounded. I suddenly wondered if there was a connection between my desire to have my neighborhood improved and the number 444. Or maybe it was just that I had somehow received some insight into what was going to be happening to my neighborhood before it happened. Did this number represent something extremely powerful? Was this power trying to impress me? Maybe it was trying to tell me something from this experience? A hundred questions went through my mind at once and my curiosity about this number was overwhelming.

I started to silently ask questions. I said, "Someone, please tell me what is going on here?" And then I said "What is going on in my life? I need to know!" But still no answer. No revelation. I received no understanding, whatsoever, about what was happening to me with this number.

I continued to wake up at 444 a.m. and stare at my digital clock. Even though this was becoming routine, every time this happened it still caused a deep sense of wonder in me. Why was this happening?

MY DEMONS AND DREAMS

During the four years that I spent in New Hampshire, I continued to see the number 444 on a regular basis. I had almost gotten used to this, although I still wondered what it all meant. So far the 444 sightings had been fairly odd, but nothing terrible had come from them. I was still confused about whether or not this was a good thing that was happening to me or a bad thing. Quite honestly, I could not make sense of it. It seemed to me that I was involved in something that was beyond this world, although it did seem to be directly affecting my life from time to time. It was when some very strange things started happening to me that my life took a turn for the worse. It was then that I started to believe that this was a bad thing that was happening to me.

It started one night when I was having a bad dream.

I still can't remember what the dream was about. But when I suddenly awoke from this dream and opened my eyes there was an image of a demon right in front of my eyes. The image of this demon seemed to last for a couple of moments and it did not go away, even when I was awake with my eyes open. The image of this demon would just not go away no matter where I looked. I even rubbed my eyes, but this demonic image was still right in front of me. There was also a feeling of complete terror that accompanied the image of this demon. I remember that this demon was hairy in appearance with big teeth.

When the image of this demon finally disappeared from my sight I was very relieved. The extreme fear and terror that I felt also seemed to fade away. I sat up in bed and rubbed my eyes again and did not know what to think about what had just happened. I did not feel like going back to sleep anytime soon so I sat there in bed for quite some time wondering what had just happened. How was this possible? How could a demon appear before my eyes right when I woke up and then remain there for me to see while I was awake? This had never happened to me before. Any nightmares that I had ever had before were over as soon as I had opened my eyes. This was very frightening to me to say the least. Little did I know that I had just entered a period of my life where I would be seeing more demons and having more dreams.

I don't remember the order in which they appeared, but I do remember what most of the demons that appeared to me looked like. They usually had big teeth and a very menacing appearance and they always struck a chord of intense fear and terror deep within me. They seemed to appear at random intervals; anywhere from a couple of weeks to a couple of months apart. The same demon never visited me twice. It was always a different looking demon but with the same feeling of terror. This was the kind of terror that seemed to be on a very deep level. The image of these demons would always stay with me for awhile, even after I was awake. I can say that I never got used to seeing these demons. They were also never associated with the number 444. I never woke up at 444 a.m. in the morning when one of these demons seemed to appear in front of me. So while there was no association between the number 444 and these demons, both things were happening during the same period of my life. Once again, it felt like I was going through an extremely bizarre period in my life.

Another thing began to happen too. I began to have some very interesting dreams. These dreams were always very colorful and I could always remember them in great detail after I woke up. Many times I would have these dreams right before I would wake up. These were the kind of dreams that would stay in your mind for days. They would leave you thinking about them and wondering if there was any deeper meaning to them. Were these dreams actually premonitions of things to come? Were these dreams of things that had happened to me in the past, possibly in a past life? Or were they just very vivid dreams of things that my mind wanted to experience?

I remember one dream in particular. It occurred in the year 1999. With the changes that have taken place in our world today it's hard to imagine that, in 1999, things around the world were quite different. The global situation was very different than what it is today, more than ten years later. But in this dream, I had dreamt that the United States of America had launched a pre-emptive nuclear strike on Russia. It was a quick dream, but I remember seeing a missile heading for the city of Moscow in this dream, and then orange and red flames before my eyes as I woke up. I also remember very distinctly, someone whispering in my ear as I woke up, "Where are you going to go?" I sat up and looked around only to realize that I was alone.

This dream was very strange to me because it seemed totally impossible that the United States of America would ever do something like this. It was also very strange to me because of what had been whispered in my ear as I was waking up. The words, "Where are you going to go?" went through my mind. This was strange. Also, who was it that had whispered this in my ear. Was it an Angel? Was it some spiritual guide? I wondered about these things because I had never heard anything whispered in my ear like that ever before when I was sleeping. It just seemed to accentuate how strange my life was becoming with all these dreams and demons and other bizarre things going on. In fact I was becoming very depressed and didn't know what to do or who to turn to for help.

I realized that there was really no one that I knew that I could turn to for help. I had tried to relate these things to my wife and a few other friends. But I could tell that they were as baffled by these things as I was. No one I talked to could seem to give me a good explanation as to why these things were happening to me. Some people would say, "You're just having some bad dreams". Or they would say, "Maybe you're just under a lot of stress." They all said things that were true, but they were not able to understand that what I was going through was a serious spiritual crisis. I didn't even realize this at the time, but I did know that I wanted things to get better in my life. I wanted an explanation for what was happening to me. But things continued on and seemed to get even stranger.

THE SYNCHRONICITY OF IT ALL

I began to realize at this time that other things were happening to me as well. I began to experience a certain synchronicity in my life that played itself out in different ways. It started out simply and eventually became very complex. In the beginning I began to see things like the same word several times in a short period of time. I remember seeing the word "Swift" several times in a row one morning. On this particular morning a car pulled right out in front of me and slowed down so that I was forced to concentrate a little more on this car in front of me. Inevitably, whenever this would happen, I would always look at the license plate of the car in front of me. There it was, the word "Swift", right in front of me. Within a few seconds of noticing this word on the license plate of the car in front of me, a big truck drove past me on the other side of the road. On the side of its long trailer was the word "Swift", written in large letters. Wow! Was this a coincidence? Why did this happen? All I could think about as I drove home was the word "Swift". Was something in my life going to become Swift? I knew what the word meant. But what, if anything, did this word have to do with my life?

For the rest of that day I kept thinking about this word. Why did I see this word twice in a row in such a short period of time? It gave me the same feeling I had gotten when I first started seeing the number 444. I just knew that this word meant something in my life, but I wasn't sure what. It wasn't until I picked up my daily prayer book that I began to understand what this was all about.

I had recently bought a prayer book that had a daily prayer in it for every day of the year. I would read this book every day and enjoy the daily message that it had for me. I had not yet read this particular day's daily prayer. But when I did, it really left an impression upon me. It was about God's help and how Swift His help is. This daily prayer let me know that God's help comes to us very quickly when we need it. This really left an impression on me. I knew that this word would be important to me because of the way that I had seen it earlier in the day. And then I saw it in the daily prayer that I read a few hours later. It's hard to explain how this word just jumped off the page when I read it. It was kind of like experiencing the same type of feeling that the number 444 left upon me every time I would see it. I just knew that this word was part of a message that was directed towards me. In this case it was a very positive message.

This started to happen to me in many ways. Sometimes I would see other words that I knew were important. But the explanation of the meaning of these words in my life would not always come to me as quickly as the word "Swift" had. Sometimes I had to wait several days before I would understand what a word might mean, or the message it carried with it. And then I would see the word written somewhere and understand its meaning. It was as if the word that I saw several times in a row would become a marker for me to look for. Where would I see this word, or marker, again? Would it be in a magazine article or maybe in a book? Sometimes I would hear an important word, or marker, in a movie or television show. I began to realize that there was usually some type of message in these movies, shows, or books that pertained to what I was going through in my life at the time. I began to call this type of synchronicity and the meaning that it brought into my life, "a message from beyond."

But who were these messages from? Why were they coming into my life? The meaning of the message about God's Swift help was quite obvious to me, even though my understanding of God and my faith in

God was not that great, at this point in my life. But it was pretty obvious that the word "Swift" was tied into a message about God and His very quick help that He gives us when we need it the most. Things weren't always so clear though. I was also receiving messages that seemed to be very disturbing, almost as if they were from another source, other than God. Could these messages have been from some evil source, possibly the devil, himself?

There was one day when I was driving in my car and I saw the word "Look" on a license plate. Just like the word "Swift", I thought that this was a very interesting word to have on a license plate. I didn't know the reason why the word "Look" was on the license plate of a car that was in front of me when I was driving. I just kept thinking to myself, "What could this word mean?" I remember it was just a few minutes after seeing this word that I arrived at a four way intersection with stop signs. Another car was approaching the intersection from my right and I was expecting this driver to stop as well. Since I had already come to a stop at this intersection I proceeded to drive forward. However, the car that was approaching me from my right did not stop at the stop sign that was in front of him. In order to avoid an accident with this car, I blew my horn and stepped on my brakes.

What happened next is hard to describe as far as

how it made me feel. The car that I was trying to avoid, came to a screeching halt right in front of me and the man that was driving this car gave me a look that scared me to death. It was a menacing look and he just sat there looking at me for what seemed to be a very long time. Who would do such a thing? I thought to myself, "Who would drive through a stop sign, slam on their brakes in the middle of the intersection and then just sit in their car staring at the person that they almost hit with their car?" Apparently this man would. Eventually he continued driving on and so did I. But the feeling that this man gave me by looking at me made me feel just like those demons did when they seemed to look at me in the nighttime. I was terrified. Then I remembered the word that I had seen just a few minutes before I had encountered this man whose look seemed to terrify me. Look.

Was this word a bad word? I never thought so before. But how had this word carried a message right into my life through the man that had been driving the car that almost hit me? It was as if a different type of energy or a different force had gotten me thinking about the word "Look". What was the message behind the word "Look?" It seemed to be a very fearful message. But what did it mean? I never really figured out the meaning of that very frightening event, other than it seemed to send a terrifying feeling right into my soul.

But there were also other times that I had very terrorizing messages come to me from beyond. And sometimes the message was very clear. Death; war; burning; hatred; and many other messages as well that left me feeling depressed, lost, and without hope. Quite honestly I felt like I had somehow entered hell itself, even though I was still alive, right here in this world.

UPS AND DOWNS

Throughout this strange period of my life there were many ups and downs that I never thought were possible. Eventually I began to realize that there were many unexplained things that were happening to me. Some of them were very good and some of them were very bad. It was almost as if two opposing forces were at war and my mind and soul was their battlefield. I remember thinking that it felt as though I was going through an "Armageddon at the level of the soul". I had been so torn apart by these forces that, at times, I had no will left to live. I realized many things during this time though. It was as if I was learning about spiritual things at a very accelerated pace. This really took a toll on me mentally and spiritually and ended up really bringing me down at times. Usually when I felt depressed and worn out, bad things seemed to happen to me. I would either see another demon in the night or I would see a license plate that read WW III (World War 3- really saw it) and I would think to myself, "I think this world is coming to an end, soon."

But then there were times when magnificent things would happen to me. These were things that would help me continue on with my life. Like when my first daughter was born. It was the greatest thing in the world to me. And I will never forget how I found out that my wife and I were going to have a baby. It was in 1999 and I was sitting in a flight attendant lounge. This lounge was available to flight attendants who needed a place to sit for a while when at the airport. I had five hours to sit in this lounge on this particular day before I had to work on my next flight. I had actually fallen asleep for a while when I was awoken by a voice on the intercom saying, "Trip number 444 will now be briefing in the conference room". This was not my trip number, but nonetheless I had just heard the number 444 loud and clear. I then looked at my watch and it was 444 p.m. "Here we go again", I thought to myself.

I then called my wife who was at our home to say hello to her. When she answered the phone she immediately told me that we were going to be having a baby! I couldn't believe it. She had just found out herself. Since this was going to be our first child I was incredibly happy. Then I remembered how I had just heard and seen the number 444 twice before I called my wife. This was incredible. It was almost as if this number was saying to me."Get ready for something really awesome!" And it was absolutely awesome when our first child was born. She was to become a very important part of my life, along with her sister who was born two years later.

But the bad things seemed to continue too. I remember becoming obsessed with the dream I had had about the preemptive nuclear strike against Russia by the United States. It brought an uncontrollably unsettled feeling to me. It made me feel like I had to do something about the possibility of this actually happening. Not knowing what else to do, I actually started to write to the President of the United States by sending e-mails to his e-mail address. "This is crazy", I thought to myself, "he will never read these e-mails because he is probably receiving thousands of other e-mails a day too". But I sent him the e-mails anyway.

I think it was in 1998 and 1999 that I sent the President my e-mails. I wrote him about the cruelty of war and how we should be trying to create more peace in this world. I mentioned that we cannot create peace in this world by using military force. I also mentioned that we, in the industrialized world, needed to help those who were living in extreme poverty in third world countries. I tried to explain that every day innocent children were dying from hunger. I mentioned that these children were also dying from diseases that could be easily cured, but there was no medicine available to them. I tackled other subjects as well. I wrote to him about how I thought there were many things that needed more attention so that the level of suffering in this world could be reduced, or better yet, ended. I actually received a few form letters from the government in the mail, most likely generated by a computer. But this was to be expected.

After a year or so of writing the president I began to realize that I was not going to accomplish much by sending these e-mails to the President. I silently acknowledged to myself that this world and all of its wars and famine and mismanagement would probably continue on forever. It was the way of this world and I would never be able to change it on my own. I think this was a huge turning point in my life. For once in my life I began to realize that I was going to have to put my faith in something else besides the president of the United States, or any other powerful worldly figure for that matter. I also began to realize that during this time I had been neglecting my own health. Could it be that I was more concerned at the time with the condition of this world than I was with the condition of my own physical, mental and spiritual health?

I also thought it was time to begin putting my trust in something other than worldly institutions. Whether it was a government, a stock brokerage firm, or some other worldly institution, I thought it was time to stop depending on these institutions for what I needed in life. I decided it was time to humbly ask God for His help instead of looking to these worldly institutions for the help that I needed. It was the humbling process that I needed to go through in order to ask God for His help that was very difficult for me to go through, though. Up until this point it seemed to me that so many crazy and unexplainable things had been happening to me that I thought God could not seriously be involved in my life in any way. Other things, that I have not mentioned, had also happened to me that were almost evil in their nature and outcome. And it was the overall sense of hopelessness, despair, lack of love, and deep depression that I was experiencing that was preventing me from reaching out to God.

But somehow I broke through this prison of despair and acknowledged that I needed God's help in order to break free of the strange and evil things that were happening to me. One day I actually told God that I loved Him and I think I turned another corner that day. I don't know why, but this was a very hard thing for me to do. It was almost as if every fiber in my being was saying, "You don't really believe in God, much less love Him, do you?" But I said it anyway and after I said this I began to feel much better about my life. I think it was at this point that my relationship with God really began. Many messages had come to me about God and Jesus in the past few years but I did not take them to heart. In fact it was the negative messages that seemed to influence me more and had a greater effect on me in a very negative way.

THE CROSS

Before I had encountered the number 444 I had never really thought about Jesus. I had gone to church when I was younger and still living with my parents. It was there that I had learned about Jesus. However, I had really only considered Jesus to be someone who was a central figure in the bible. I had never really contemplated His teachings and I didn't really ever think about Him or pray to Him. Whenever I was going through a tough time in life I just weathered the storm by myself and waited for things to get better. And they usually did get better; until I began seeing the number 444 and had many strange things start happening to me.

It was after a couple of very difficult and very strange years that I began to realize that my life had seemed to have changed forever. These strange things that started to happen in my life were apparently going to continue with no end in sight. This made me feel very depressed at times and also very isolated, as if no one else could possibly be experiencing what I was experiencing. My depression only got worse and there were actually times when I thought about ending my life. I had never thought about doing this before in my life and it was quite evident that things were not going very well in my life. I had entered this period of my life gradually with the "444 sightings". Then things seemed to pick up speed. I started to see demons and have very vivid and bizarre dreams. I also had an unexplainable sense of doom and depression that had encompassed my whole life. Why had my life become like this and when would I ever get back the life I had once enjoyed? It almost seemed as if something had hijacked the life that I had once enjoyed.

One day, as I was sitting in a chair at home, a thought occurred to me. I remembered how a few days before this particular day, I had seen a girl who seemed to be very happy. I saw her when I was at work, as a flight attendant, on a plane. She smiled readily and seemed to be a very peaceful person. She seemed to have a normal life and did not seem to be depressed or sad at all. I noticed how she was wearing a cross on a necklace that she wore outside her shirt. I remember how I had kept thinking about seeing this cross on her necklace. I took this to be a sign that she believed in Jesus. I didn't know what religion she might have believed in or if she had even attended any church. All I knew was that she was happily wearing a symbol of Jesus around her neck.

As I continued to think about this I realized that I too could be wearing a cross. Maybe this would help me in my fight against this seemingly endless despair that had gotten a grip on me. I thought to myself, "I can just go down to the Bible store and get a necklace with a cross on it and wear it around my neck." I felt very excited about this prospect and decided to immediately go down to the Bible store that was in the town that I was living in at the time. As I tried to get up out of my chair and head to the Bible store, a sudden unexplainable feeling of depression came over me. It was almost as if someone or something pushed me back down into my chair. Immediately there were negative thoughts racing through my mind. It was as if a voice in my head was saying, "A cross is just a symbol and it won't help you". Some of these other thoughts seemed to say to me, "Nothing is going to help you and you know this".

I remember just sinking down into my chair and experiencing that awful feeling of depression again. It was almost as if my soul was sinking down into hell. Why wouldn't a cross help me? Why did the girl who had been wearing a cross around her neck seem so happy? Since she had been wearing a cross around her neck, I had thought that maybe this was why she was so happy. Was the cross she was wearing a sign that Jesus was protecting her? And had this girl been saved by Jesus? The questions continued to race through my mind. But the last question that entered my mind was the most difficult. Why had I been unable to get up from my chair and go to the bible store and purchase a necklace with a cross on it? It felt as though something was definitely not allowing me to do what I wanted to do. It wouldn't be until much later in my life that I would realize that at this point, metaphorically speaking, I was taking the long way home.

GOD

In my life before the 444 "sightings", believing in Jesus was one thing, but believing in God was an entirely different thing. I don't know why this was. Possibly it was because I could believe that there had been a man named Jesus who had walked the earth over 2000 years ago. But I still had trouble believing in God, mostly because I had no idea who God was. God had never spoken to me directly, nor had God identified Himself in any way to me. Consequently, I did not know if I believed in God. I wanted to believe in Him very much sometimes. But there were other long periods of time in my life during which the thought of God never went through my mind.

I had gone to Sunday school and church when I was being raised as a boy and I had learned about God from the Bible and other books as well. But what I learned in church had not stuck with me in my life and the older I became the less I seemed to think about God. There were times in my life that were very difficult. There were also times in my life that were very fun. I thought I had been leading a fairly average life, filled with life's normal pleasures and disappointments. I had never made a million dollars in my life or won the lottery. But then again, I had never had to do without the things that I needed in life. I thought my life was pretty average and I thought that this included not thinking much about God.

It wasn't as though I had anything against God or religion. It was just that I seemed to have no need for it at all. I was fairly self-sufficient in life and everything that I needed seemed to come to me. It wasn't as if I hadn't earned my living in life. I had always had a job in life and I always felt like I was doing fairly well in life. I never went without food, shelter or friends. These were all very important things to me in life and I had them all. There was no need to pray to God or to ask Him for anything in life. I was not rich, but I had what I needed. That is, I had what I needed until my life started falling apart physically, mentally and especially spiritually.

I remember one Christmas when I was hanging ornaments on our Christmas tree. During this particular Christmas season I was feeling very depressed and almost completely drained of energy. At this point in my life I had been seeing the demons and having the strange dreams and was definitely experiencing some type of spiritual information overload. Except all the information that had been coming to me lately was very negative information. It was really taking its toll on me mentally, physically and spiritually. Until this part of my life, I hadn't realized that not all things spiritual are good things. And I was beginning to realize that there was a lot of evil out there in the spiritual realm. I was seeing things that I had not seen before in my life. It was frightening me and wearing me out. Feelings of extreme isolation and hopelessness were starting to set in and these feelings only intensified over time. It seemed that there was no one to turn to and it also seemed like these negative feelings were here to stay in my life.

Even though I had very little energy, I decided to try and hang a few Christmas ornaments on our Christmas tree. After a few minutes went by, I remember accidentally dropping one of the Christmas ornaments that I had been hanging on our Christmas tree. The glass ornament hit the hard wood floor with a soft shattering sound and spread across the floor in what seemed to be a thousand pieces. "It was such a pretty ornament", I thought to myself. But now, it was gone forever, shattered into a thousand pieces. Instead of immediately cleaning it up, I sat down in a chair and stared at the shattered ornament. It seemed to glisten in the light. It was then that I realized something. I realized I was actually staring at what my life had become. At least I was staring at what I thought my life would look like if someone could actually understand my life. It was a shattered mess. I had reached a point in my life that seemed like rock bottom. It felt to me as if my very own life had been dropped and had been shattered into a thousand pieces. How would I ever put my life back together?

For some unexplained reason, I suddenly imagined that God was watching me right at this very moment. I imagined Him actually watching me look at the shattered ornament that lay before me on the floor. Then I imagined Him thinking the same thing about my life and how it had seemed to have fallen apart into a thousand pieces. I wondered if He was sad? Just like I was sad looking at the pretty ornament, now shattered. I started to wonder about what God might think of my life. Was he possibly looking at me, now that I had fallen and my life was shattered? Was He wondering if I would ever be able to put my life back together? Little did I know that not only had He been watching me my whole life, but He was actually going to be calling me in His own way. God would be calling, but what would He want?

It wouldn't be until much later in my life that I would finally understand that He was actually calling me. But I had gotten to the point in my life that I was actually enthralled with the idea that God might somehow be coming into my life. I had reached the bottom and was ready for anything that would get me back on my feet. I just didn't realize at the time how it was going to happen or how God was going to be calling me. All I knew was that in the past few years my life had been filled with things that were only depressing me; things that were of a hellish nature. To be honest I didn't even know if some of these things were from God Himself. There were times when I thought to myself, "Why is God letting this happen to me? I must have really upset Him somehow". Other times I thought, "I can't imagine that I need to straighten things out with God." This was a pretty scary thought.

But when God finally did call on me, it was a very gentle thing. In hind sight, He was calling me from beyond, at a point in my life when I truly thought I was walking through hell itself. It really was as if He had been watching me fall and when I finally hit the bottom and shattered, He wanted me to know that He was there. He wanted me to know that He loved me and that He would help me if I would only let Him into my heart. His calling was a gentle calling. He did not knock my door down with force. That had already been done by something else. Rather, He was letting me know that His help was available, but I had to ask for it. This is the way He would work in my life. Even though I was soon to be amazed at the power that He had, God chose not to impress me with it by knocking down my door. He would impress me soon enough with things that I had long since forgotten about like Love, Hope, Joy, and other beautiful things. These would all slowly come back into my life once I had let God back into my life.

LESSONS

Why did many spiritually scary things happen to me? I have thought about this throughout the years since my spiritual crisis started happening to me and also since it has seemed to have truly lessened and turned into something much better in my life. This very scary spiritual time in my life seemed to be a gradual escalation of negative spiritual events that culminated in a completely frightening experience. It's not as though I was terrified all the time, but there were obviously moments when I was completely out of my comfort zone and left wondering what was going on with my life. I have to admit that I had very little experience with spiritual matters before any of the frightening spiritual phenomenon started happening to me. I had attended church when I was growing up as a boy, but this seemed to do little good with the situation that I found myself in. It seemed to me as though some type of force, other than God, had taken control of my life. There were stretches of time when I would seem to regain control over my life, but then as soon as I would be able to enjoy this time, it would seem as though this negative force would assume control of my life again.

It seemed as though a battle was taking place in my life. I remember thinking that it almost seemed as though the devil himself and God were battling over my soul. Maybe this is what was actually going on. In hind sight I actually feel as though I was also being warned about what is out there in the spiritual realm. I believe that the things that I experienced were things that I learned immense amounts of knowledge from. But I also think these things that I experienced comprised a certain type of warning about what the future could hold in store for me if I did not change the current spiritual path that I was on.

There have been times when this idea seemed a little farfetched to me, though, because I always considered myself to be a good person. I was employed as a flight attendant for a major airline, I owned a house that I was remodeling at the time, I was married and was starting a family, and I thought I had really done nothing wrong in my life that would deserve such attention as the type I was receiving from beyond this world. When I reflected upon my years as a boy and as a teenager and then as a single adult, I could not come up with anything that I had done that was so terrible that I might be going to hell when I died. Actually the idea of hell itself never really entered my mind and was the furthest thing from my mind when I was a young adult. I really didn't think I was that bad of a person.

However, it seemed as though the universe or some higher power had a different impression of me. I wondered why this was? Had I done some things that I shouldn't have done in my life? I knew that deep within me there were things that I wished were different with who I was. I could get angry at times, I could be stubborn at times. And there were times in my life that I had frequented bars and indulged in the lifestyle of the late night crowd. I had also stolen a candy bar from a store one time when I was just a young boy and I had fought with my two brothers when I was growing up as a boy. And as a young man I had also had a tumultuous relationship with a girlfriend. I had also lied to people about things that I didn't think were important. I had gotten into some fights before, and there were other things that came to mind when I really contemplated what I could have done wrong in my life.

What I didn't realize though is that I had been breaking spiritual laws without even knowing it. How could this be so? What kind of laws could I have been breaking? The answer to these and other questions would come to me eventually. Over time I realized that it was the basic beliefs in life that I had as an individual that would be challenged by a higher force. I was actually like a house of cards that was going to be hit by a spiritual storm. Or like Jesus said, "A house divided cannot stand." But how was I like a house that was divided? This answer would eventually come to me and once again, over time, I would realize that it was my beliefs and principles in life that would be severely challenged and ultimately changed by the spiritual storm that I was going through.

"Turn the other cheek." These words went through my mind from time to time when I would contemplate why my life was in such turmoil. Other words of wisdom or spiritual advice that I had heard through the years would also pass through my mind from time to time. Eventually I began to really contemplate these words of wisdom that would come to me. For example, during this very difficult spiritual time in my life it seemed to me that humanity itself had turned against me for a time. There was a period in my life when people in general seemed to be very angry at me for many reasons; reasons I could not understand. Whether it was when I was at work, at the grocery store, or maybe driving my car somewhere. People just seemed to go out of their way to show me how angry they were at me, or so it seemed. These were people that I did not even know. My reaction was usually to get angry right back at these people. I thought that if someone was going to be getting angry at me, then I had the right to be angry at them.

These encounters never turned out well and I was usually left with a very negative feeling about these people and about myself. Sometimes I could not stop thinking about these encounters for hours or days. They seemed to leave a very irritating impression with me about how people could be. But then the words would come to me again. Turn the other cheek. I thought "Turn the other cheek?" Why? Was it not my right to be angry at someone if they were angry at me? "Turn the other cheek."

It was during this time in my life that I was reading books that had to do with spirituality. It was in these books that I discovered some very powerful messages that I began to use in my life. And it was through these books and also through my experiences that seemed to synchronize with the messages in these books that I began to learn some very important spiritual lessons in life. I began to realize that if I did "turn the other cheek" when I was confronted by an angry person, I was acknowledging that I did not want a confrontation with them. Even more importantly I was saying to God, "I am going to leave this situation in your hands." The outcome of these potentially angry situations became much different when I decided to "turn the other cheek" and not react to an angry person in my life.

There were also situations that would arise from time to time when I would perceive that a person had done something wrong to me. Whether it was someone who stole from me, somehow, or someone who had lied to me about something, I would find myself rushing to judgment about the person who had done something wrong to me. I began to realize that I could use the same principle of turning my cheek to people who I thought had wronged me in these situations. Some very amazing things began to happen when I decided to do this. These difficult situations seemed to just work themselves out, sometimes miraculously, as though God Himself had designed the outcome. I began to realize that turning the other cheek and then praying to God for His help was the most powerful thing that I could do in life when I felt that someone had done something wrong to me or was angry with me.

Other lessons would come to me as well. I seemed to be constantly learning about new ideas that seemed to make little or no sense to me until I contemplated them and then actually put them to work in my life. These lessons usually started out as a message of some sort and often times seemed to be of a negative origin. It wasn't until I really thought about my life and realized that there were things that I needed to change on a spiritual level that these messages would seem to make sense. I apparently had to learn many things in life.

Another lesson I had to learn was when to stop "banging my head against a wall" when I thought that something needed to be done or accomplished in my life. I needed to learn to stop trying so hard to accomplish something and instead hand it over to God. "Just let go". These were some other words of wisdom that seemed to fit perfectly into this lesson. I had to surrender my will to God and accept His will in my life. And no matter how hard these lessons seemed to be, I was always learning them for a very good reason- to let God help me in life. These lessons that I was learning had to do with undoing some very stubborn blocks in my belief system that seemed to be blocking God's help from entering into my life. I knew that God wanted to help me in life, but many times I did not know why He did not want to help me when I truly needed His help. It was very hard for me to realize that I was the one who was blocking His help or His plan for me in life.

ON LOAN

It wasn't until later in my life, when I had time to reflect, that I realized that all of the evil things that had been happening to me weren't necessarily from God. In fact they weren't from Him at all. But since I had not formed a very strong relationship with God in my life before this very stressful time, I did not realize that not everything that had happened to me was from God. It was just like the story of Noah and the Great Flood. I had been taught in Sunday school that it was God who had flooded the earth because He was angry at the world. He then told Noah to build an ark and prepare for the Great Flood that would eventually kill everyone except for Noah and his family and the animals that he brought with him. I think I subconsciously carried with me in life this story and how it portrayed God as an angry God. This type of thinking, that God was somehow angry from time to time with me or possibly other people that I knew, or read about, had somehow influenced what I thought about God.

And when I started to experience some very negative things in my life, things that I would call pure evil, I started to think that maybe God was very angry with me. I thought that there were some serious things that I had to get straightened out with God. And while maybe this was partly true, there were also times that I thought God had totally abandoned me while I was in harm's way. But what I didn't realize was that God was right there with me while I was going through the worst time of my life and He really only wanted to help me. I now know that God understood that I did not like the way that He was apparently not helping me in the way that I wanted Him to help me. But He also knew things that I did not know and these things involved some pretty tough lessons that I needed to learn. However, at the time, I still did not realize that He was with me the whole time that I was learning these lessons.

What I also didn't realize at the time was that I was actually on loan to another force- the devil himself you might say. As improbable as this may seem, it was actually another force that was trying to impress me and dominate me through very negative means. This was a force that was not aligned with God and a force that had evil intentions. This would make sense to me later on in my life, but because I did not have a very strong relationship with God at the time, this evil force was allowed to run wild with my spirit and my soul. It entered into my life through my mind and then became engrained in my spiritual being through the negative impressions that it left me with. There were moments when things would flash through my mind that were of a very negative origin. I would see images that were very disconcerting and would instantly put me on a fearful path. Instead of praying to God, I would remain impressed by these seemingly evil things and would continue on in life with the feeling that nothing could be done about this.

There were times when I would actually ask God to help protect me from these evil things. I had very little faith in God at the time, so my prayers were more like questions at the time. I would ask God, "Why are you not helping me?" And when these negative things would continue on in my life I was left with the impression that God truly did not exist or that, at the very least, He did not want to help me. My life had become so bad that there were times that I had decided that it would be best if I just ended my life. But somehow I chose not to do this. I think it was a message about death that went through my mind one day that really left an impression upon me. It made me rethink the possibility of taking my own life. I realized one day that even if I were to take my own life, I would only continue my existence in another place or dimension, where I had left off in this life. That is to say, I realized that if I left unfinished spiritual business in this world, it would find me in the next. That is the way the devil works. If there is unfinished business, he will find you no matter where you are, in this world or the next.

This may sound scary that the devil will find you no matter where you are, and it certainly was at the time to me. But I realized one thing. I was going to have to confront my demons and all of the other fears that I had in me on a spiritual level, either in this lifetime or the next. This realization was the one thing that kept me going and prevented me from taking my own life. It didn't make me feel any better about what was going on in my life in a negative way, but it did keep me going so that I could confront my demons with God's help. I believe that this was a message, or realization, that was sent to me by God. For without this bit of knowledge I would not have made it through the very evil ordeal that I was going through that seemed to have no end in sight to it.

However, I still did not realize at the time that I was "on loan" to another force. It was as if I was on loan to the devil, but in a certain way. The devil himself was being allowed to impress me in a very negative way. It seemed as though he had hijacked my life, for good, and was sending me down a certain path towards hell. Or maybe it was that he had just plain thrown me into hell. But either way, I was experiencing things that I could not explain as to why they were happening to me. It wouldn't be until much later that I would realize that although the devil seemed to have control of my life, I was still being protected by God and His Angels. Even though I was literally seeing demonic images right in front of my eyes, I was also being protected from their full force in my life, by God. And although this was a very terrifying time in my life, I was being protected from actual harm by God, Himself. There were some times though that harm would actually seem quite imminent. Whether it was a close call on the highway while driving, or a close call on an airplane while flying, or any of a number of other things that seemed like they could have been very serious in a negative way, God was always protecting me.

One thing that I had forgotten during the most troubling time in my life was that God had created my soul, spirit, mind and also my body. There was no way that another force that was unaligned with God would be able to do harm to me, because God owned me. However, there was one thing that allowed me my freedom to experience other things that might not have been the best things for me to experience- my free will. This is also what God gave to me when He created me. My free will allowed me to accept another force into my life without God interrupting this. If I had been praying to God more diligently for His will and not my own will, then I may have been a lot safer on my spiritual journey. This then was my conundrum; I didn't have the strongest relationship with God and so it seemed very easy for me to become involved with a very negative force in life. This force has many names, but the devil comes to mind when trying to describe this negative force.

It truly was my free will that allowed me to wander from the protection that God offers us every moment of every day. That is why I feel that I was "on loan" to the devil. God was still protecting me, but He was letting me experience many things in life that He wanted me to experience, if I chose to experience them. These were very negative things as well as positive things. In the end, after I had experienced enough things on a spiritual level, I was able to choose which spiritual path I wanted to continue on. I believe that I chose the right path when I started to pray to God for His will and for His plan to come into my life. It could be said that it was His plan to allow me to see many things that really frightened me on a deeper level. But it was also His plan to let me "come back" to Him in time, when I had decided that I only wanted His will, and no one else's. I suppose I had seen enough of the negative side of life and spirituality and was only interested in seeking out what God wanted me to do. I thank Him every day for allowing me to come back to Him and enjoy His Love, Joy, Hope, and Protection. The extent of my fear and depression that I experienced at times parallels the words that Job speaks of in the bible; "...thou scarest me with dreams, and terrifiest me through visions: So that my soul chooseth strangling, and death rather than my life."

FORGIVENESS

God's forgiveness is a wonderful thing. It is invaluable in that people may very well need it every day of their life in order to continue on with the business of everyday life. If a person thinks hard enough about what they may have done in life that was not in line with God's will, it could be very hard to continue living a normal life. The fact that many people have done some things in their life that may have been hurtful to other people or to their self is a normal fact of life. But it can be very hard for people to think about some of the things that they have done in this life that they would rather not have done. It is for this reason that God offers us His forgiveness in life. He understands that many people in life will somehow "get off track" or partake in what many people call sin. It is very possible that we have all done something in life that we would rather not remember. Or perhaps we wish that what we had done had never even happened.

This is when God's forgiveness becomes invaluable to us. We must realize that we cannot continue on doing the things in life that are hurting other people or ourselves before we can really accept God's forgiveness. But if we concentrate on those things in our life that bring about negative results, we can hopefully correct these things and then go straight to God's forgiveness. This is how we can also experience some very negative things in life that we may have brought upon ourselves, but yet still have the means to continue on with our lives. There is no limit to the expediency, or speed, with which God can forgive us. His forgiveness is immediate. But this does not mean that we can continue on living our lives in the same way that we were living them when we got into trouble in the first place. In fact if we choose to accept God's forgiveness in our lives it may actually mean that we need to seriously fix a part of our lives that was responsible for the trouble we got into in the first place.

If we choose to do this, then we are accepting what God has planned for us. We are accepting the fact that we will be trading in our will for God's will. This may also mean that we may have to "come clean" in order to accept God's forgiveness. How can we "come clean" in our life? The process of "coming clean" can actually take a lot of time in our lives to complete. If we decide to accept the plan that God has for us in our attempt to "come clean", then we are accepting the personal responsibility that comes with accepting God's plan. His plan may involve many things for us. These may be some very hard things that He may wish for us to accomplish. Many times these may be things that will change who we are forever. And with that being said, it can only be imagined that some of the things that He may have planned for us could be very difficult things.

It is truly with hard work that we can change who we are in life. If we continually take the easy path in life we may be missing out on some very difficult times in our life. But we may also be missing out on some things that could change us for the better in this life and also in a spiritual way that would not only make God very happy, but ourselves as well. Without the challenging times in life that can bring about true spiritual change we may never rid ourselves of the vices, negative habits or self-destructive ways that we may have come to embrace in life. And without ridding ourselves of these negative things we may not be able to accept God's forgiveness.

Some people may be able to continue on in this life without needing God's forgiveness. At least this is what they may think until they experience a very deep negative event in their life that would ultimately point them in the direction of God and the forgiveness that He offers. The types of negative experiences that a person can experience are unlimited. It could be of a physical nature, spiritual nature or possibly something else. But the result will most likely be the same. The person experiencing a deep negative event in their life will seek help where help can be found. Some people may turn to doctors or prescription drugs for help. Some people may turn to alcohol or drugs for help. Still other people may turn to psychiatrists or psychologists for help. Most of the time these things can either help people or offer them some type of escape. In fact many people do very well with these things over the course of their lifetime.

But it is when none of these things will help, when tried by a person that we can get into a spiritual jam. By this it is meant that we may decide to try certain things in life that will offer us "guaranteed" help or escape, but sometimes these things may not act as planned. The result that we expected from these things is less than what we wanted or needed. This is when things can seem to get scary. It is also when a person may decide to turn to something that they would not normally have turned to for help. And this is when many people may decide to turn to God for His help, when all else has failed. And God will not fail us. Only we can fail ourselves by not accepting God's help and forgiveness. The best thing we could do is to accept the plan that God has for us, no matter how difficult or impossible it may seem to be at first. Because not only is anything possible with God's help, but His help may also be the only thing separating us from our demons and our own personal hell. Once this is realized, the decision is usually pretty easy.

MORE DEMONS

As I mentioned before, my experience with demons started one night when I awoke from a bad nightmare. I do not remember what my nightmare was about, but as soon as I opened my eyes, there was the image of a demon right in front of me. It did not matter if I blinked or rubbed my eyes, the image of this demon would not go away. It lasted for what seemed to be five or ten seconds, or to someone who had never experienced this before, an eternity. This demon was accompanied by a deeply terrifying feeling that seemed to go away when the demon disappeared. I will never forget this particular night when this happened and it left an impression on me that I can still recall. This is when I realized that my life had changed forever. Even though, at the time, I did not realize that I would be visited by more demons in the future, this one demon was already enough for me.

"Why did this happen", I thought to myself? I also remember thinking to myself, "This is impossible". I had never heard of this happening to anyone before. Even though I had seen horror movies in my life that had demons in them, I just thought it was plain crazy to think that a demon could ever appear to anyone like this.

I don't remember if I slept anymore that night or not. But I do remember thinking about this demon a lot. I didn't tell anyone about this because I thought for sure that they would think I was crazy. And that is exactly what I thought was happening to me at the time. I thought I must be going crazy. Well, then it happened again. I saw another demon a few months later. There was just enough time in between the two "demon sightings" that I had stopped thinking about the first demon that I saw. This is why the second demon almost scared me more than the first one. I thought maybe the first demon was just going to be an isolated event. But this next demon was proof enough to me that I was either going clinically insane or that something out of this world was beginning to happen to me. I chose to believe the latter. Although at this point insanity was not a bad option.

It goes without saying that I felt desperate. On the one hand, if I were to obtain the help of a psychiatrist or a psychologist, I am pretty sure that the diagnosis would not have been a good one. On the other hand, if I had sought out the help of a church minister or priest, I am sure that they would have deemed me possessed. And although the eventual outcome of either of these options may have been a positive one, for all I knew, I decided to ride out the spiritual storm that I was in, by myself. Even the thought of taking some type of prescription drug to ease my anxiety about these demonic sightings entered my mind. But I still decided to go through whatever I was going through on my own without the help of a prescription.

It was one day when I was listening to a song on the radio that I began to get some insight into what was going on in my life with these demons. I remember I was driving to work one day, listening to the radio. The song on the radio had some lyrics about a devil woman. I don't remember much else about it, other than I was listening to the song very loudly. While this song was playing, I ended up pulling up to a red light behind a car that had the letters "Devil Wmn" on its license plate. I remember staring at this license plate while the song about a devil woman was blaring on the radio. "O.K., I'm insane", I thought to myself. I drove to work that day in a kind of stupor that only someone whose life is crumbling before them can really understand. But it got worse.

That afternoon, when I was finished working at the airline, and was at my layover taking a nap at my hotel, another demon visited me. I woke up from my nap and there she was, right in front of me; a beautiful woman, but with very scary features. She even had the menacing teeth that so many of the demons had that were visiting me in the night. I just sat up and stared at her for what seemed to be a very long time. Wow… This was starting to get out of control. No one would have believed me if I told them that I was listening to a song about a devil woman on the radio, and that I saw her name abbreviated on a license plate, and that I actually saw this devil woman as I was waking up from a nap later that day. This was obviously the strangest experience I had ever had. The fact that I could tell no one about this gave me a very depressing feeling. I was going to have to figure this one out on my own.

In time, I began to realize that these demonic images actually represented demons on a different plane of existence that were trying to enter into my heart, mind and soul. They were also trying to break my spirit, in an attempt to control me through fear. I also realized that some of these demons were demons who had been with me for a long time. They had been trying to influence the decisions that I had made in life in a negative way. But they were finally making themselves known to me. I also began to realize that if I concentrated on what these individual demons looked like, I could usually pair them with a part of my life that was less than perfect, spiritually. In fact some of these demons actually looked like areas of my life that needed immediate spiritual attention.

Several months after this devil woman visited me, a demon appeared to me after I had been angry earlier that day. I remember he was the angriest demon I had ever seen. Then it occurred to me- I must have felt just like this demon earlier in the day when I was very angry. This was very interesting to me. I began to realize that maybe this particular demon was influencing my anger. That is to say, I began to assume that maybe this very angry looking demon was responsible for triggering episodes of anger in my life. Yes, it is true that we all have to be responsible for our emotions in life. But it was at this moment that I realized that I was receiving negative interference in my life by demons, or forces, that were not aligned with God. Sometimes it was almost amusing to me to see which demon was going to be coming my way on any given night. But other times it was downright depressing.

I remember when my first child was born. She was the greatest thing that had ever happened to me and the greatest thing that had ever come into my life. When she was born, I was staying at the hospital in a room with my wife. We each had our own bed and my wife was very tired after giving birth to our daughter. So at one point, when our daughter was crying, I picked her up and held her in my arms. I too was very tired, so I put her down in her crib and lied down on the bed. After a short time of sleeping, I was awoken by a terrible jolt to my system. I sat straight up in my bed and opened my eyes. There was the image of the devil himself, right in front of me. He was laughing, but he was also very terrifying in his appearance. He looked just like how the devil himself, is usually portrayed as looking; red face, a tail, and horns. The timing of his appearance and the fact that this demon seemed to be the devil himself, terrified me. And that is really an understatement. I began to realize that this was not some sort of game that I was playing, where I was trying to guess what type of demon was going to be appearing to me next. In fact at this point I began to feel very depressed about what I had just seen.

But it was my daughter herself that would ultimately help me out of this hellish experience. I wouldn't fully realize it until later in my life how much of a positive influence my daughter and her sister would have on me in my life. She was my first child and I had yet to experience the unconditional love that a child can bring into a person's life. She and her sister would end up becoming my anchor in what was the worst storm that I could ever imagine going through. They were truly a light in the darkness. I would end up realizing later on in my life that God had truly blessed me in the darkest of times, by blessing me with my two beautiful daughters. I began to realize that God was there with me, in His own way. It was a way that would, once again, be a very powerful, but yet gentle way. This is when my love for God began to grow immeasurably and it was also when the tide had finally turned in my favor.

A SPIRITUAL CRISIS

I am not going to lie. When I started to see the number 444 over twenty years ago, I thought that this was a strange and wonderful thing. At first I remember thinking that it was kind of a cool thing that I was seeing this number so often and I thought many things might happen as a result of this. I remember thinking that maybe if I played the number 444 in the lottery, I would win some much needed money. I also thought that maybe I would somehow be able to impress people with my stories of how I was seeing this number. Neither of these things ended up happening though. I never ended up playing this number in the lottery, and all of the people that I mentioned this number to seemed to think that it was pure coincidence that I was seeing this number so often. I am sure that these people probably thought other things as well. I can just imagine what they were saying about me when I would tell them that I was seeing a certain number in my life and that I just knew that it meant something.

But things progressed at their own pace and soon I was seeing other things that were like "444 sightings", but of a more negative slant. The things that I started to see seemed to be of a very evil nature. I must say that I did see some very good things during this time, but it was the more negative things that seemed to get my attention and really left me with the impression that something had either "hung me out to dry", or that I was under some type of spiritual attack from beyond. It was a really confusing time in my life. Things which I had neither heard of nor seen before began to happen to me. It seemed as though there was nowhere to go in order to escape these negative things that were happening to me. In this life, you can run or drive really fast if you need to get away from something quickly. But in the spiritual world, this is impossible. Especially if you are not even sure what it is that you are trying to get away from, or how to do this.

I was left on my own to figure out what was going on in my life and why such negative things were coming my way, mostly in the spiritual world. Although, there were many times when the negative things I would see in the spiritual world would translate directly into my life in this material world. This happened with positive things as well. But there was a stretch of years that I went through that were very difficult years. During these years it seemed that there was no end in sight as to when these negative things would stop happening to me.

There were also books that I read at the time that seemed to give me either a very negative spiritual experience, or a very positive one. I could only tell whether a book that I was reading at the time would provide a good or bad experience simply by reading it and then seeing what the information in the book would bring into my life. It was kind of like downloading spiritual information from beyond and then seeing what type of effect this information was going to have on my life in this world, and also what type of effect it was going to have on me spiritually. I remember thinking to myself, "I wonder what this particular book is going to have in store for me if I read it?" It got to the point sometimes, where I would actually wonder if I should read a book that seemed to have come my way or whether I should just dodge the opportunity. It was almost as if I was shell shocked by all the negative spiritual information that was coming my way.

I didn't realize it at the time, but this was a time in which I was in a full blown spiritual crisis. It was as if

I was in a small dingy out at sea and a huge storm was coming my way. There was no escape. I could only go through this storm with as much courage as I could muster. It seemed as though there was no help at times. With every book, magazine, newsletter, or article that I read that brought negative information into my life, it was like another gale force gust of wind had blown through my soul; making the spiritual storm that I was going through even worse. How much could I withstand without "going off the deep end"? This thought ran through my mind constantly.

There were books that brought very positive information into my life as well, though. Whether they offered just a bit of encouragement, a positive message, or even some type of insight into what I was going through, these books or articles were always a welcome reprieve from the spiritual storm that I was going through. In fact if I had not gotten some very positive information at times during this difficult time of my life, I don't know if I would have made it through this difficult period of my life. It seemed that there was always something positive coming my way and it was just a matter of discovering it. I told myself that if there was a book that I was supposed to be reading, then I would somehow find it in life. I had a friend who once told me that whenever he was "supposed" to be reading a book, the universe would see to it that he would get the particular book that he was "supposed" to be reading. He said that one time he was walking through a book store and a book literally fell off of a shelf, right in front of him. He bought the book and read it.

I have never had this happen to me, but all of the books that I was supposed to be reading certainly did come my way in interesting ways. There was very little doubt in my mind as to when I was supposed to be reading a book. The only thing that perplexed me, and sometimes depressed me, was when a book that I was sure that I was supposed to be reading turned out to be of a negative source. But in the end it was apparently necessary for me to have read each book that I read. I should also mention that the forces that were operating in my life at the time had very clever ways of reaching me. There were many times when I thought that a book that I was going to read would be a very positive one, but actually the opposite would end up happening. It would turn out to be a more negative book in my life. I think many of the books that I read were not so much "negative" books, but it was the way in which they had a negative effect on me that was, at times, very interesting. Everyone has their own unique experience in life and there were times when I thought I had picked a rose, but ended up with only its thorns.

And so it was with the number 444. I seemed to be very intrigued with this number at first, but as the journey into my spiritual crisis deepened my first impressions of this number seemed to change. There were times when I wondered if this number was actually a very evil number. But there were also times when something good would happen to me in my life that I could somehow associate with this number. This would become very confusing to me over time. Was this number a good thing or a bad thing in my life? Maybe I should have been looking at it differently and in not such black and white terms. But I had heard from other books that I had read that this number represented some very good things. Was this number really associated with the angels? Was it really a sign from God Himself? Then why was I experiencing so many negative things during the time that I had been seeing this number on such a regular basis. And the fact that I had not read a book about any of the negative aspects of a number like this one only seemed to confuse me even more. I felt like I had been given a definition of the number 444 through the books that I had read that was very confusing.

If this number was indeed associated with the angels and with God, then why did it feel as though I was going through hell itself, courtesy of the number 444? Maybe I was going through hell itself and this number was a representation of the help that I was receiving from God and my angels. Or maybe this number represented something else. Could it have represented a spiritual doorway that I had opened into the spiritual world? If this were the case, then I was quickly learning that there were both good spiritual things and bad spiritual things that could come my way after I opened this door. Or maybe this number represented more of a warning about what types of seriously negative spiritual things could enter into a person's mind and soul, both in this life and the next. Maybe this was a warning about hell itself. If I were to experience some very hellish things in this lifetime, maybe this experience would push me in a different direction; a direction that was more oriented towards God Himself. Or maybe this number represented a connection to all of these things, and more, at once.

One thing is sure to me though. I would not want to ever go back to the place I was in for those years in my life when I was experiencing such negative things. The sheer terror that I felt at times was enough for me to fully embrace the relationship that I had with God which was getting stronger each day that I spent in my spiritual crisis. I suppose that it was necessary for me to experience all of the negative spiritual things that I experienced in order for me to get to "safer shores". And once I felt that I was in a safer place, I would never want to venture out into stormy waters ever again. And at the very least, if I were ever forced out to sea again, I would have a very strong faith in God and would rely on His very powerful protection that is available to all of us.

I do feel that what I went through was a very necessary thing for me to experience. But it wasn't without much confusion that I confronted what came my way on a spiritual level. I began to realize that I was going to have to discern for myself, what type of spiritual information was good, and what type of spiritual information was bad. It would only be through reading the books that I read and then experiencing the information that they offered to me on a spiritual level, that I would be able to actually determine if they were good for me, or bad for me. Had I realized that negative information doesn't just come from negatively entitled books, I would have been far ahead of the game. I had to experience the fact that there were some books that contained negative spiritual information for me that actually had a positive spiritual slant to their titles.

However, I suppose it was God's plan for me to have experienced the negative and the positive. It was His plan for me to see the darkness and the light. And I would be surprised to see how much all of this information that was coming my way actually had to do with the changes that I was going to have to make in myself on a very deep spiritual level. And in the end, this would help me to survive the spiritual crisis that had engulfed my whole life.

CHANGE

Change can come in many different forms in our life. It can be both negative and positive. The ironic thing is that we must sometimes go through some very negative things in life in order for us to get positive results and this can be a very confusing thing. When we are going through a negative experience in life it can seem like what is happening to us in life is all wrong. If our negative event that we are experiencing in life is bad enough, we might even consider calling it an "evil event". These "evil events" may seem to come from out of the blue with no warning and may seem to have no end in sight to the length of time that they will be with us. However, this may be a very necessary thing to happen to us in order to bring about the change that is necessary in each of us.

We all have things that make up who we are in life.

Most of us have positive things as well as negative things, too. But how do we know what things we have in life that are negative and could possibly be changed? And are we capable ourselves of discovering these negative things and then changing them ourselves? What negative things could we possibly partake in or harbor within ourselves? Do we drink too much alcohol or abuse our prescription drugs? Do we judge other people too quickly? Do we have a lot of anger in life? The list could go on and on. And what about the justifications that we have that allow us to continue doing the things or thinking the things in life that are bad? When we really think about it, most of us continue to do things pretty much the same way we've always done things, on a day to day basis.

But what if we were able to see ourselves more objectively? What if we weren't given a choice to do this either? What if we were forced to look at the negative things in our life that make up a part of who we are? Most of us don't even consider the fact that there may be things in our life that could be changed; or that should be changed for that matter. Many times only God knows of these things in our life. It has been said that only God knows a person's heart. For this reason alone, it may only be God that can truly help us in life when it comes to changing who we are.

But change can be one of the most difficult things in

life to embrace. The process of changing can be very, very difficult and most people when confronted with the possibility, would rather continue on in life in the way that they are used to living. But once again, what if we were not given the choice of whether or not we wanted to change? What if God decided it was time for us to compare our life to His ideals or principles that He has laid out across His spiritual world? How would this happen? Would He simply say to us, "It is time to change, so please do this now?" Would this even be possible for us to do? In many cases this may not be possible.

Instead, what if God showed us what we needed to change in ourselves in a way that would get our attention? What if this was in a way in which we had no choice but to experience, even though it might be a painful experience? And what if the change that we needed to make in our life would help to end the painful experience that we were going through in life? This could bring about change that was lasting in our life and that would impact us in a very positive way. It could be that we would have to stop doing some things in life that were destructive to ourselves or someone that we know or love.

So why would God make us do something like this or go through something that was painful? Maybe it's because we actually wanted to experience this in this lifetime. Maybe it's because we decided on a different level, even before we came into this life, that we needed to change who we are spiritually, in order to become more in line with God's will. This could only help us become better spiritual beings and also better people in this world. There are so many negative things that we, as humans, do in this world, that we could all use God's help in our lives.

But God's help may not come to us exactly how we would want it to, or envision it coming to us. It would be wonderful to win a large sum of money in a lottery, or to have a job that would pay us a lot of money. It would also be wonderful to always have the things that we needed and wanted in life. However, these things might not have anything to do with how God would want us to change. They might bring added comfort to our lives, but true comfort lies in the presence of God's Love and Protection. For those of us who have weathered, or are weathering, a negative spiritual storm, or crisis, this is a true fact in our lives. So, once again, there could be added comfort in the fact that we are doing well with material things in this world, but it is the comfort that we so desperately need in the spiritual world that can only come with true spiritual change. Yes, we can go bankrupt in this world, but we can also go bankrupt in the spiritual world as well. And this is when we need God to help us the most.

One way that God can truly help us is by helping us

make major spiritual changes to who we are on a deeper level. It may not be an easy journey, but God and His angels and guides will be there for us, if we just accept them into our lives through prayer. If we pray to God, He will answer our prayers in time. Whether it is immediately, or in some time from when we first pray, God will answer. We must also try to accept His answer for what it is- an answer from God. Whether we like it or not we should embrace God's answer to our prayers as much as possible and also remember that God has only our best interests in mind. These may also be long term interests as well. And although change would be easier if it involved short term answers to our prayers, change often involves long term answers, or answers that take some time to understand.

We must understand that change does not happen overnight and that it also often involves our participation. If we have the will to change something in our lives immediately, then we will have a better chance of changing that part of our life. If, however, we decide that we would rather not change something in our lives that maybe God has pointed out to us as something that we may need to change, then we might have to go through a long period in our life in which a long term struggle could occur. This struggle is usually within our self and at a deeper level than what most people can readily understand. It is on a level that involves many spiritual things. Demons, angels, dreams, visions, and intuition are just a few of the things that we may encounter on our deeper spiritual level. At first these things may seem frightening, but if we can accept the fact that these things are all a part of the change that is going on in us at a deeper level then maybe we can more readily embrace the change that is needed in us. It is when we keep encountering the more negative things on this deeper level that we have to ask ourselves, "Am I really trying to embrace the change that God is calling for in me? Or am I just hoping that these negative things will go away sometime soon?"

How do we know what things need to be changed in ourselves? Maybe we should "listen" to the clues that God and His angels are giving to us. It is through synchronicity (a coincidence of the extreme), intuition, dreams and visions that we can determine what areas of our life we should change. Negative events can also point us in the right direction. And change can readily occur if we can just identify what areas of our life we should be trying to change. When we know what it is that we should be changing in our life, we should then pray to God for His spiritual healing power to enter into our lives. We should also diligently work to bring about change in our lives by trying our hardest to abstain from destructive habits, vices and thought patterns.

MY TEMPLE

The wine spilled across the kitchen floor. I had just knocked my wine glass off of the table in front of me and I remember staring at the mix of broken glass and red wine on the floor. I had already had a few drinks before this and I thought that another glass of red wine would taste good to me. It was the way in which the glass fell, though, that really caught my attention. I had somehow gently brushed the glass with my elbow and it began to teeter to one side. I thought maybe it wouldn't fall if I could just catch it. But as soon as I tried to reach for it, the glass fell on the floor.

It seemed as if time was suspended for just a moment as I watched this whole thing unfold in front of my eyes. It was almost as if something was drawing my attention to the falling glass. After the glass had hit the floor, I looked up at the empty wine bottle and thought to myself, "No more wine for me tonight." It's hard to explain, but it was almost as if something was trying to cut me off from my indulgence in this sometimes nightly ritual. The odd way in which the glass fell to the floor gave me the impression that something else was involved with this part of my life. It wouldn't be until much later that I would realize that something really was trying to cut me off, not just from this habit, but from other habits as well.

There was the time that I ordered a double latte coffee drink from a popular coffee establishment and the receipt for the drink and muffin I had ordered was $6.66. I thought about how this number was considered to be the "number of the beast", or the devil, in the bible. It actually made me smile, because I didn't really think that this purchase was in any way related to the devil.

However, it was through a series of synchronistic events that I experienced shortly after this, that I began to realize that the coffee that I was drinking in the morning and the wine that I was drinking at night were literally tearing apart my body, or "temple", as I call it. On top of the toll that these drinks were taking on my body, I was also waking up and going to bed at odd hours. My work at the airlines was comprised of very long days that averaged between ten and twelve hours a day, not to mention getting to and from the hotels that I was laying over at. After nearly a decade, all of these things were getting the best of me physically.

I didn't know it at the time, but they were also getting the best of me mentally and spiritually, as well. And it was during this time that the most negative events of my spiritual journey were starting to happen to me. It was as if I was caught in the crosshairs of a spiritual crisis and my physical, mental and spiritual defenses were all down. Had I known this at the time, I most likely would have stopped my self-destructive habits and shored up who I was. By this I mean that it would have been best if I had been as ready as possible for the task that was at hand.

When my first child was born, another huge responsibility was also added to my life. My wife, who was also a flight attendant at the time, was flying "opposite schedules" with me. This meant that I was taking care of our daughter by myself for three days at a time. When my wife returned from work she would then take care of our daughter for three days, while I worked. We were also living in a house at the time that needed to be completely renovated and remodeled. We had been working on this house for quite some time and it was starting to weigh heavily on me, just knowing that we had a long way to go before it would be finished.

The amount of stress in my life was starting to

approach a level that I had never before experienced. I didn't realize though that there were things that I could have done differently during this time that would have made a huge difference in my life, and in a positive way. I had no control over my spiritual crisis and what I was experiencing. But I did have control over my own physical health and I was choosing to abuse it, in a way. In part, I was drinking the wine in order to relax at night. But this was actually making me more tired than I would have been, had I chosen not to drink at all. Inevitably I would wake up feeling very tired and would then drink a huge cup of coffee and several more throughout the day. This vicious cycle that I was caught in was literally draining my life energy out of me. I had been able to handle this lifestyle in the past, but it was when I started to "experience" my demons, that I should have been as physically, mentally and spiritually ready as possible.

If I had paid more attention to what I had been putting into my body, or "temple", I probably would have been much better off. I probably would have been able to weather the spiritual storm that I was going through, much better. But instead I had decided to continue drinking wine and coffee and abusing my "temple" with an abundance of alcohol and caffeine.

I realized later on, after the peak of my spiritual crisis had passed, that my body was really the temple in this world for my spirit, soul and mind to reside in. And when I was abusing my temple, it was not as strong as it could have been. I realized that if I had taken better care of my temple, my mind would have been clearer, my spirit would have been stronger, and my soul would have been safer.

I also began to realize that if I had been in a stronger position to weather this spiritual storm, my negative spiritual experience may not have been as difficult. At least my perception of it may have been a little more positive. There was no doubt that I had to learn the spiritual lessons that I needed to learn. But it may have been much better for me if I had been residing in a stronger temple; and if that part of me that was connected to God was better able to remain connected to Him.

POWER

All power comes from God. If we believe anything else, then we are subjecting ourselves to the influence of other powers that seem to lurk in the spiritual world. Along with believing in the power of your choice come the advantages or disadvantages of that power's influence on you. We can always take a chance and try to believe that there is other power in the universe and in our lives besides God's power. But this belief may actually end up harming us in the long run and in ways that could leave a very lasting impression on us. Even if we link ourselves unknowingly to a negative source of power, it won't be long before we may start asking ourselves if we are being served by a power that has the best intentions for us. If we try to project our own power, or what we perceive to be our own power, we may also end up in a situation that is less than perfect. So when it comes to power, what should we do?

Jesus was one of the most powerful individuals to ever walk this earth. There were people living during his time that knew of his power and they were obviously so impressed by it that they assumed that he was here to lead them into battle against whatever it was that was oppressing them at the time. Maybe it was the Roman empire, or maybe it was King Herod's legions that were leveling a certain controlling power against the people of Jesus' time. But whatever it was that was oppressing the people of this time was going to have to wait for another man to confront it. For, Jesus was here to confront a different power that resided in an unseen world- the spiritual world. He was here to show us that we could be released from our demons and be healed as a result, by using our faith in God. Jesus used his power in a way that was very positive. He did not use his power, or the power that God gave him, to inflict personal injury, or to conquer other nations. He instead used his power to heal people and to show them the way into the kingdom of heaven. He never chose to impress people with his power. Instead he spoke in parables to show us the way and used his healing power to try and better the lives of people that he came in contact with.

Could we try to do the same things that Jesus did?

There is no doubt that this would please him very much. If we all tried to use the power that we have in a positive way in our life, this world would no doubt be a better place to live in. But there could be times when we feel the urge to strike out against someone in our life in a negative way. We might choose to use the power that we have to impress someone or possibly hurt that person because of the hurtful feelings that we may be harboring towards them. However, if we were able to stop our impulsive negative behaviors, when it comes to the power that we may have, we may find that we could instead heal a relationship, or show someone something positive about themselves with our power.

We may ask ourselves, "What kind of power do I have in life?" The answer to that question might surprise some people very much. We all have the power to persuade people if we choose to do so. We also all have the power to make people feel good about themselves, as well as bad about themselves. And there are many other powerful things that we have at our disposal, that can either help someone or possibly hurt them. It is all in the way in which we choose to use our power that really counts in the end. It is wise to remember that whatever we "put out there" will "come back" to us in time. It may come back to us immediately, or it may come back to us later on in life. And if we believe that we live many lifetimes, than what we "put out there" could very well "come back" to us in a future lifetime.

In the end, Jesus' use of power was to show us how we can become better people, both in this world and in the next. He also made a promise to us. He promised us that if we believed in him, we would ultimately experience the kingdom of heaven. He made no exceptions to this promise and even said that, "Only through me shall you know my Father." By this, it is meant that if we follow Jesus and believe in his teachings and his ways, we will experience the kingdom of heaven. Could this also mean that if we do not believe in Jesus, or at the very least, follow the spiritual principles that he laid out for us, might we experience something else other than the kingdom of heaven? The answer to this question is very possibly so. Turn the other cheek, not my will but God's will, love thy neighbor as thyself. These are all very important spiritual truths that Jesus taught us. If we violate these truths, then we are deciding that maybe it is best to follow the principles of another power. And yes, Jesus could definitely be considered a power to be reckoned with.

If we follow another source of power other than God, which Jesus exemplified, than we are choosing to follow the principles of that power as well. If we choose to believe in another power, then we will be served by that power and its principles. The best litmus test that we can take, is to ask ourselves how we feel about some very important things in life. Are we frightened of certain things in life like death, war, disease, or other negative things. And how are we able to cope with, or confront these things in life, if we are not certain about what the power that we believe in has to say or do with these things in life. We can be certain that with Jesus, and a sound faith in God, these things will not prevail over us in this lifetime. We will also be saved in the end if we believe in Jesus. This was a part of his promise to us and we can rest assured that he will deliver on his promise.

The interesting thing is that we can experience some things right here in this lifetime that we can be saved from with our faith in God and Jesus. Our lives can take some pretty interesting turns that may seem to come to us from "out of the blue". And it is during these sometimes negative turns in our life that we need to be saved from our sometimes seemingly negative or hellish experience. It is usually just a matter of time before we understand that we are truly powerless in this world when it comes to things that are of a very deep negative spiritual origin. But if we can just choose the right power to put our faith in, we can then choose to be saved by this power- the power of God.

ANGELS

Angels are very powerful beings of light. Like Jesus, God's angels have been empowered by Him to protect us. Just like parents, angels know what is best for us and God entrusts His angels to look after His children. It is when we find ourselves in dangerous situations that our angels protect us. It could be a dangerous situation that we know of or it could be a dangerous situation that we may have no idea about. It is often times the danger that we cannot see that our Angels tirelessly protect us against. God has many ways in which He can protect us from danger and His Angels are on the front line of our every day defenses against evil.

Another way in which our angels can help us out is with spiritual growth. We have all come to this world for our own reasons and many of us are here to learn more about our spiritual selves and our relationship with God. This is where our angels can help us. They can act as intermediaries in our lives between God and ourselves. God is talking to us all the time, but are we missing His message? Our angels are here to make sure that we get God's message, as long as we are paying attention to our angels and to what they are trying to tell us. They may be pointing us in a certain direction in life. Sometimes this may be a new and possibly confusing direction that needs to be mapped out for us. How can this be done for us?

Our angels are very good at mapping things out for us. Whether it is a new direction in life that we should be taking or maybe it is just a message that we need to hear in order to start understanding the spiritual things that we need to understand in life. The messages that may come to us from our angels are messages that may vary in meaning and intensity. How important are the messages that are coming our way? One way to find this out is by listening to our angels and then determining ourselves how important these messages may be. It is true that all messages are important, but we may begin to go through periods of our life in which some very important messages will come our way. And it is in the way that these messages are delivered to us that may very well determine just how important they are.

If we get a message over and over again, it is quite

possible that this is a very important message that is headed our way. No matter what the message may be about, we should definitely take heed of the message. Even if it is a message that we don't particularly want hear, we should listen to it and then determine what it is that we should be doing with the message. Many times if we are in some type of danger we may get a message about something that might scare us. However, once again, we should pay attention to this message and then act accordingly. These messages might show up as a dream, or a daytime vision, or through words or phrases showing up in our lives with synchronism. We should listen to these messages and then determine what it is that we are doing in our lives that could be changed, so that we can avoid any type of danger that might be headed our way.

Danger might come in many ways. It could just be that we are not as close to God as we should be and our angels are trying to get our attention and let us know this. It could also be that something we are doing in life is putting us in danger. What could it be and how should we change the things that we are doing that could be putting us in danger? We should simply keep listening because our angels are sending us messages all the time and they will be sending answers to the questions that we may have, as well. Always keep paying attention and you will see the messages as they come. They may be few and far between at times, and they may come constantly at other times.

Our angels also have many other types of messages for us. They can be our greatest source of support at times. When we find ourselves depressed about things or in a negative mood, don't be surprised if a very positive message about our life should show up. These positive messages may be about us directly or maybe about something that we do in life that is of a very positive influence on others. Messages like, "Hero, I love you, Best friends, Excellent, Good job", or anything else may come your way and in a very positive way. These could all be messages that we get from time to time and they are usually messages that we need to hear in order to keep our spirits up. It is true that sometimes we need to hear some negative things once in a while in order to get our attention about things that need to be changed in our lives, but we need to hear just as many positive things in life in order to keep us going on a day to day basis.

Positive messages are our angels' favorite thing to deliver to us. They know that these messages will make us feel good about ourselves, and ultimately this is what the angels are trying to do- get us closer to God so that our lives are better and we feel better about ourselves. Our angels know that we may have to do some very serious spiritual work in order for us to get closer to God, but they are there for us and are ready to do whatever it takes in order for us to become closer to God. It is with great enthusiasm that our angels try to get our attention by sending us messages, especially positive ones.

Our angels also work for us "around the clock", literally. When we look at a clock and see a certain time on it, we might think that our angels are trying to connect with us. And this is not far from the truth. Our angels have many ways in which they are trying to connect with us and numbers are just one way in which they can impress upon us that they are right here in our lives, "twenty-four, seven." There are other ways in which they may try to connect with us. There may be other symbols that they choose to use in order to connect with us. They may simply choose letters as a way in which to communicate with us. Some people may ask, "How could an angel use letters to communicate with me?" It may take a while to understand the meaning that a symbol, or letter, may have, but it is entirely possible to grasp the meaning behind the symbols that our angels may be giving to us. It is through diligently paying attention to the messages that come our way from time to time, that we can begin to understand the meaning behind a symbol. Once we understand a symbol's meaning, then we can start to better understand what the angels are trying to tell us.

We may see a symbol over and over again, and then we may see a word or a phrase right after seeing this symbol that seems to stick out to us. Maybe it is this word or phrase that actually could be attached to the symbol that we have been seeing. If this is the case, then it is safe to assume that the symbol that we have been seeing may actually have a new meaning attached to it. A symbol could be anything. It could be an actual design or a picture of something or even just a letter of the alphabet. Don't be surprised if you start "collecting" symbols and their meanings over time. This is one of the best ways that our angels can then communicate with us.

A symbol's meaning might be anything that is important to us and our angels. Some meanings may have a more negative slant, but this is so that our angels can warn us about things in life, if this should be necessary. Many meanings may have a positive meaning behind them, and still other meanings may have little to do with our lives until we experience their meaning at the right time in our life. No matter how strange a symbol's meaning may seem to us, we have to embrace the fact that it may be a part of some greater message that our angels will be giving us. If we can just put together the meanings behind the symbols that our angels want us to know about, then we can really start to understand what it is that our angels may be trying to communicate to us. And this is one of the most important ways that our angels can communicate with us- with the use of symbols.

Another important thing that angels can help us with is improving our spiritual lives. Our angels are the gatekeepers to our soul. It is when our soul or spirit may seem to be under attack by negative forces that our angels can really help protect us. It may be when we feel the negative influence of something that does not have our best intentions in mind that our angels can stand steadfastly beside us, protecting us from evil. If we find though, that somehow our angels have let us down by letting some type of negative force into our lives, we really only need to look at ourselves in order to figure out what really happened. This is because, if we choose not to pray to God and our angels, we are actually saying to them, "I don't need your protection right now, thanks." Our angels never get mad at us, but they will obey our wishes. Sometimes we may be under spiritual attack from a negative source for quite some time, and usually this is because we have been neglecting our angels by not acknowledging their presence in our life.

If we always thank our angels for helping us in life and pray to them for their guidance and protection, we will be sure to have this protection from them for the rest of our life. Even if we just pray to God on a regular basis, our angels are very, very happy, because they then know that they have done their job. They know that they are here to serve God and His children and when His children thank God for His protection and guidance, they are really thanking God's angels as well. But it is always important to thank our angels for everything that they do for us in life.

ANGELS IN THE FLESH

There it was again. That word that I had just seen the other day seemed to jump right off the page. I was reading the bible at the time, in an effort to gain some spiritual insight into what was happening to me. All of the seemingly supernatural events that had been taking place in my life for some time were enough to drive me to investigate any source of spirituality. And the bible seemed to me to be a pretty good source. I forget which book of the bible it was that I was reading, but I do remember reading something about "being spared the rod." Well, I had recently been seeing the word "rod" in different places and within a short period of time. I started to think about this word and also the phrase in which I had just read it in the bible.

I thought that "to be spared the rod" meant

something along the lines of avoiding some type of punishment. While I could have been wrong in my understanding of this phrase, this was the meaning that stuck with me nonetheless. I thought that maybe I was in some way being "spared the rod" in my life. What was it that I was being spared? Was it some type of punishment for something I had done? I was really trying to figure this out, as I was very interested in what could possibly be coming my way if I were not on my best behavior, spiritually or otherwise. It seemed as if I were going to have to wait for the possible meaning behind this word, as it was not having any particular bearing on my life at this time. Or maybe this was just pure coincidence that I had seen this word several times in such a short period of time.

It was one morning, several days after I had seen this word that I drove to a local coffee shop in the town that I was living in at the time. I couldn't wait to have a strong cup of coffee and read the newspaper. My wife was working at the time and I was off of work for the day. My first child hadn't quite arrived in our life yet, and these were times that I could still do pretty much whatever I wanted to do with my own time in life. I entered the coffee shop as usual and ordered a double cappuccino with a muffin. It wasn't long until I was seated and was enjoying my coffee and muffin. The news was pretty much the same as it always was in the newspaper that I was reading. In fact everything was pretty much the same as it usually was at this coffee shop, on this particular morning; that is, until a certain man walked through the front door of the coffee shop.

He actually kind of weaved through the front door and proceeded towards the counter to order some coffee. I remember he was very loud and very direct with the person that was serving him his coffee. "Oh well", I thought to myself, "he's probably really in need of a cup of coffee, just like I am." It was after he bought his cup of coffee and turned to survey the coffee shop for a seat that I began to think more things to myself. "I bet he's going to sit down at the table right next to me." I was actually used to things like this happening in my life. Throughout my life, I had truly tried not to judge people in life for who they were, or what they looked like. I thought that this was a pretty good way to look at people in life and it landed me in situations in my life where I would become friends with people who were quite different than me.

Well, fate would have its way again. This particular man started to talk to himself as he moved my way. He stopped to look at one man who was seated in the coffee shop and then proceeded over to my table. He sat down at my table and introduced himself to me. The alcohol on his breath made its way across the table, "I'm Rod, who are you?" I told him my name and noticed that most of the people in the coffee shop were looking at us. Maybe it was the fact that as a flight attendant, which I was at the time, I was always used to people looking at me while I worked on an airplane that made this situation bearable to me. There was also a part of me that was very accommodating to all kinds of people in life and was very non-judgmental about people in general that made me comfortable with this man.

But what was about to happen next made my pride in the fact that I was hosting this man at my table just disappear. "Well, what makes you think that I don't know anything about people's problems in life?" It was a fair question, but why was he asking me this? He continued on and began to talk about some things that I had been thinking about lately that had to do with the spiritual journey that I was on. The fact that he actually conversed with me about my life and seemed to have the wisdom of a sage really caught my attention. I found myself actually talking to him about things that other people in my life had no interest in talking about. "This man is truly enlightened", I thought to myself. But it was the fact that he had brought up some very personal subjects that had a direct bearing on my current spiritual crisis that was starting to make me wonder just who this man really was.

How did he know what I was going through in life

on such a personal level? After all, he was the one who was offering up some very pertinent information about my life even before I had told him about what was going on in my life. It was as if he had been watching my personal spiritual crisis evolve over the past few years and was offering his advice on the matter. I remember how funny it was to me, when I finally took a break from our conversation, to see other people in the coffee shop looking at us with whimsical looks on their faces. The fact that an intoxicated man had walked into the coffee shop, right off the street, and had started an extremely engaging conversation with me, was very intriguing to these people, to say the least.

I think we had been talking for about an hour when he finally said to me, "Remember, it's who you hang out with in life that you will be waking up to in life, every single day. And if you find that you wake up in a dumpster, then you had better well change the crowd that you are running with in life." He then got up from his chair, turned to me, and said, "And you know what I am talking about." He then weaved back out of the coffee shop and into the street, never to be seen by me again.

The last thing that this man had said to me seemed to be a little odd at first. It was because he had actually been talking to me in more elegant terms before he left, and his last bit of advice seemed to come from a different part of him; a part that was more in tune with the material world than the spiritual. But it wouldn't be until I went through some soul searching later on that I would understand the truth behind his last words to me. Maybe it wasn't just the people that I was hanging out with in life, who I thought were all good people, but rather the negative forces from beyond that I had been hanging out with that really represented the wrong thing to be hanging out with in life. There were many mornings when I felt like I had awoken in hell, much less a dumpster itself. The demonic images that I would sometimes see at night made me feel anything less than good when I would awake on those particular mornings.

This man had told me many other things that could only make sense to someone who was going through what I was going through. I thought to myself, "He seemed kind of like an angel of sorts." As unlikely as it seems, that is how I would remember him for the rest of my life. There were things that he mentioned to me that actually were like answers to me that I had been seeking in my spiritual life at the time. I didn't realize what a lasting impression he would leave on me. There were many times after that when I would go to that coffee shop and look for him. But I never saw him again. To this day I truly wonder if he was an angel, or at least if he had been possessed by an angel. Could this really happen in life? Could angels speak to us through other people? Or could angels really inhabit this earth for a time and then leave, never to be seen again? I still wonder about this every time I think about my conversation with Rod.

PURIFICATION

Without purification we are but sails in the wind, blowing listlessly, as though our direction lies somewhere else than the spiritual world. Anyone can say that their goals are spiritual in nature. But it takes a soul whose spirit and nature has been purified to truly declare that they are in line with God's principles. If we think we are on the path to righteousness, than we needn't look any further than our own spiritual compass. And what is our spiritual compass, we may ask ourselves? This question has no simple answer. But the end result of a person's spirit, soul and mind that has not been purified is that of a ship that has no destination. We wander aimlessly through life trying to grasp at things that may have meaning to us, only to be disappointed when we meet with emptiness along the way.

We must purify ourselves in order to discover God's Will within us. And how should we do this? We should do this through diligent prayer and discovery. We all know what prayer is, but what about discovery? What things could we be talking about when we think about discovery? How about personal discovery? What then could we discover about ourselves that could lead us in a more God-like direction? How do we compare to God and His ideals for His children? Are we in line with his expectations of how we should be acting or thinking? And how important are the thoughts that we think about every day? Are our thoughts borne of God's ideals or the devil's temptations?

We entirely underestimate things when we think that what we carry in our minds throughout the average day is not very important. But on the contrary, what is in our minds is what we will experience on a moment to moment basis every day of our lives. This is to say that if we are concentrating on something that is not in line with what God would want us to be thinking about, then we are subjecting ourselves to the power of something other than God Himself.

This may not seem to be a bad thing at first, until the "bottom" of our spiritual world begins to fall from beneath our feet. We may begin to experience a life that is not what we had in mind- a life that seems to be out of our control and in a bad way at times. We may end up asking ourselves what has happened to our life and why we are on a path that seems filled with hopelessness and despair. We may say to ourselves, "This is not what I had in mind!" when we think about where we are in our life.

But we needn't look any further than ourselves and the thoughts that we carry with ourselves on a daily basis when we are trying to figure out what has gone wrong with our lives. For example, if we constantly think about the things that we don't have in life and then dream about how we might acquire them, we are doing several things in life that will only separate us from God and His plan that He has for us. First of all, we are concentrating on those things that we do not have. By thinking along these lines we are only compounding those fears and wants that lie deep within our minds. We are consciously saying to God and the universe that we do not have what we want, or much less than that, what we need. By doing this, we are putting ourselves at odds with God's plan for us in life.

This truth is operable on all levels in our life and for all aspects of our life as well. If we are seeking peace in our life but cannot seem to find it, then perhaps it is our fixation on something else than that which is peaceful in our lives that is causing a disturbance in our life. If we pray for God's Peace and Happiness in life, then we are going to displace feelings of anxiety and will ultimately become more purified in that area of our life.

And so it is with any part of our life. If we find ourselves "straying off course" by thinking about things that are not in line with God's Innocence and Purity, then we may have to suffer the consequences. It is not that God would want to punish us for straying from His purest ideals it is just that by entertaining thoughts that are not of the highest ideals, we are testing the waters of another force, other than that of God. And while God is the only true force in this world, we are free to assume otherwise and delve into a relationship with something other than God. It is only when we align ourselves with God and His power of Protection, that we will truly be comforted and guided in this life.

So we must try to consciously dispel any thoughts of impurity in our minds in order to become at one with God. Anything that we think about on a daily basis that may not be in line with God is something that we must concentrate on removing from our thoughts daily. And if we ever discover that we can no longer go on with our life then our demons may have finally gotten the best of us. It is when impure thoughts course through our minds on a daily basis that we know we may have been defeated in our attempts to purify ourselves and become more in line with God. It is when we discover that our life is being ruled by the demons that we harbor on a deeper level that we must consider the fact that we need God's help. How do we know that our lives are being influenced by a force other than God? Or to put it in words that carry more truth, how do we know that we have handed our lives over to something other than God?

It is when we begin to see things in our life that are not aligned with God that should immediately alert us to the fact that something has hijacked our life, or rather we have given our life over to a force that is not aligned with God. What could these things be? We need to look no further than our dreams, fears or intuitions in order to discover what it is that has taken our peaceful life from us. Visions of terror and monsters from beyond may be only a few of the things that we may encounter along the way. Our journey is sometimes not only defined by God, but by what we have ended up befriending on a deeper level.

This then goes hand in hand with the process of purification. If we are seeing things that we truly wish we weren't seeing, then it is time to purify ourselves on a very deep level. In order to accept God's Protection in our lives, we must purify, or purge ourselves of some very destructive thought patterns. The desire to drink alcohol or abuse drugs, whether they be prescription drugs or not; the desire for gratification of any sort that is not aligned with our daily needs; vengeful thoughts, whether they be justified or not; desires that seem to go unfulfilled but run rampant through our daily thoughts; wants of any material origin that could otherwise be dispelled through more thankfulness to God; the list goes on and on.

If we should ever be confused about the things that are keeping us in an unpurified state of mind then we should look no further than the source of unrest that has crept into our lives. It is only when a soul is truly tortured by the visions and nightmares of a source other than God, that this same soul will try and reconnect with the purity that God is demanding of them; a purity that resides only in the thoughts of those that are truly aligned with God and who have been awoken through the process of a potentially "dark night of the soul" or long walk through hell.

It is only when we cry out to God for His help that we realize that He has been there the whole time for us, but we have been blocking His help through the entertainment of other forces in our lives. And God would never force His way into our lives. It is rather through a possibly violent discovery, or encounter with something that is greater than our own ego, that we turn to God. This is when He is able to share His protection with us and dispel any other force that is not aligned with Him from our spirit, soul and mind. However, only we can decide when enough is enough. How many demons must we encounter along the way or how many negative events in life must we go through in order for us to surrender to God's Will and Purity? That is up to each individual. And the amount of fear and suffering that each soul decides to put them self through can be staggering, at times, before they realize that they simply cannot win their battle without God's Help.

Not everyone is subject to these standards though. In fact it may seem at times that certain people are allowed to go on with their lives in a way that is anything but aligned with God. How can these people seem to "get away with things" and still continue to enjoy their lives? Because it is only up to God to determine when a soul is going to go through a major change or "awakening" in life; and perhaps up to that soul as well, even before they came into this world. It is only when a soul is "awoken" that these seemingly terrifying things may seem to occur to that soul. And if this should happen to someone who has not had any experience with the negative side of the spiritual world, the smartest thing that this person could do is to begin the process of purification for their own sake.

Purification in the spiritual world is like taking a bath or a shower in this world. It is the process by which a person can rid themselves of any habits, vices or thought patterns that are not aligned with God. There should be no worry or confusion when it comes to purifying one's self or coming clean, because usually God will point out to us what needs to be taken care of in order for this process to begin. And if we choose not to listen to God, then there are a host of other un-Godly things that will be more than happy to begin the process for us. Either way, depending on the level of suffering that a person can endure, a person will most likely choose the path towards purification, one way or the other.

THE SPIRITUALITY OF MADNESS

There they were- dropped on me like a ton of bricks. A relative of mine had just given me some letters that my grandfather had written to my grandmother, over fifty years ago, after they had separated. It wasn't the fact that they had separated that had really gotten my attention, rather it was what the letters portrayed about my grandfather that really weighed on me like nothing else had in quite some time. They revealed something about him that not many people had known about; he had been living with a mental illness for the latter part of his life. Like many mental illnesses, it had entered his life quietly and then consumed him until his end.

Little did I know that the content of these letters would implicate me in my own dramatic schemes of spirituality smashing into this material world, or more likely, what I thought had been a sane mind. Were the things I had seen been just illusions created by my mind, or quite possibly the start of my own mental illness? Were the demons in my head just portraits of the spiritual madness that had consumed my mind, or were they somehow real?

Until I had seen these letters I had assumed that everything I had been going through was a very real experience that other people would readily believe and would somehow be able to relate to. But the letters that I was served seemed to add an eerily depressive suggestion that the demonic visions that I had borne witness to was just the tip of my mental madness running wild. The fact that maybe I was going through an experience that was somehow more mental than spiritual was crushing to me. Until I had seen these letters, I had been able to assume that I was on a spiritual journey in life that would astound everyone that I had related it to. But instead, was I truly mad? Was I really walking around in a world that my broken mind had somehow concocted, based upon the fact that I was delusional or worse yet mentally unfit?

I knew that I wasn't a danger to anyone in this world. My present attitude was a peaceful one and had somehow been a peaceful one to everyone I had known while I was in my state of mental turmoil. But what I didn't realize is that quite possibly I had been harmful to myself. My mind had very possibly gone into a state of mental illness and designed a scenario that left me scared and scarred for life- especially after I had read my grandfather's letters.

I knew immediately after reading them that anyone could connect the dots between my own terrifying, otherworldly experience, and that of a man who was mentally ill. Specifically, the fact that my own grandfather had had delusions of self-importance, persecution, and the possibility of being haunted by people or forces that other people did not know or could not see, sent a shock of despair through my being. I could no longer even refer to my being as my soul. Nor could I refer to the experiences I had gone through as being evil. I could only look upon my experiences as those of a delusional man that had experienced something other than a dark spiritual journey.

But what if there was some type of spirituality in my madness? What if there was a genuine link between me and the other side of this world? Why hadn't my grandfather mentioned anything about God or the devil in his letters to my grandmother? It seemed as though he was only concerned with the forces or people that he imagined were after him and wanted to destroy him. I could relate to him in this respect, though, remembering the things I had gone through that seemed to point to my own destruction, or want thereof. But what if this destruction was actually a type of personal destruction that was being orchestrated by my own mind? What if the terrible things I had seen were all due to my genetic link to my grandfather?

The thought of this was unbearable, mostly because of the fact that before reading these letters, I had framed my dark experience in strictly spiritual terms. I had previously blamed the devil himself, or my own lack of spirituality, for the horrible things that had happened to me during my dark journey through hell. I couldn't understand how my dark experience could be anything less than spiritual, much less something relating to a mental illness. But all the signs and symptoms pointed to the hallmark of a mental illness infesting my mind. Even the fact that I had seen "messages" concerning future events that would take place in my life could apparently be explained by a mental illness.

And after researching the devastating signs, symptoms and effects of illnesses like schizophrenia, I began to feel darkly enlightened (if I can use that term) to the fact that I was mad. It was plain and simple according to the research I had conducted. Everything I had gone through could be attributed to a man whose mind was not healthy. All of the dreams and images I had seen, even in my waking hours, could be explained by a mental illness. I felt as though my hard earned spirituality had been shattered; just like I had felt ten years earlier when I had dropped a Christmas ornament on the floor. It was now pure madness and nothing made sense like it had before I had read my grandfather's letters.

But I thought to myself, "What about the spiritual insights that I had fought so hard to understand and ultimately categorize in my mind?" Were these, too, a part of a mind so torn by mental illness that no sense could be made of them any longer? And why did these spiritual truths I had learned still make sense to me if I chose to believe that, somehow, I was not mentally ill? Or maybe there was some sort of connection to my madness with spirituality? So many questions ran through my mind. It seemed as though my whole spiritual experience had, at the very least, become an even darker blend of madness and spirituality.

I remember how I had thought that what I had gone through for all those years meant nothing to me now. It was as if I had gone through a type of mental madness and somehow come out the other end, after a five year rampage through hell. I knew that things had somehow become better in my life. But now I could only explain this by thinking about how I had somehow come out from under the dark shadow of a mental illness. My research even indicated that people with mental illnesses could many times escape their illness spontaneously. My research also indicated that they could slip back into their illness, in time, as well.

So how would it be with me? Would only time be able to tell as to whether or not my madness would return? Or was I truly free of the dark madness of my mind for good? After the apex of my dark experience occurred, I began to see less and less of the truly frightening things that I had experienced before. I had originally thought that maybe this was because I had attained a sort of spiritual balance and understanding in my life that had somehow freed me from my hellish bonds. But now I was entertaining the possibility that it was madness, itself, that had brought me into the most terrifying, albeit enlightening, part of my life. Could it be, though, that there was some sort of mental mix in my mind that involved madness and spirituality?

My greatest hope now was that the things that I had seen during my dark spiritual journey were actually borne of the spiritual world. That would mean that I had truly encountered my demons in this three dimensional world. It would also mean that I had seen many other spiritual things that many people would assume were pure madness, but they would be wrong in their assumption of this. And how ironic this hope of mine was, considering at one point during my dark journey I thought how madness itself would have been a better option than the terrifying things I had seen. I remembered how some of the things I had seen were so frightening, that to assume that they actually existed was an option that was less enjoyable than madness itself.

So once again, how was it going to be with me? Would anyone else be able to answer my questions concerning the madness I had endured? And would I even want to hear their answers?

A DIFFERENT LETTER

There it was- spirituality again. And this time it was in a much needed place. The letters that had been given to me that my grandfather had written also contained a different letter from his brother. It was written to my grandfather and contained the type of information that only an enlightened soul would be able to write. It was a letter that was designed to give my grandfather a much needed boost in his sinking morale. It was also intended to enlighten my grandfather to the possibility that his current state of mind was one that was not entirely "at one with God."

There were references in this letter to God and "our Master" in which my grandfather's brother was trying to wake my grandfather up to the fact that we are actually spiritual beings having a material experience in this world. The fact that my grandfather had "gotten off track" over the years in his lifetime was very apparent to his brother and his letter was not short on directness, but was also laced with eloquence and references to spirituality, as he saw it.

But little did my grandfather's brother know that his letter would have a profound effect on someone else, over fifty years after he wrote it…me. I really needed that letter. It was like a beacon of light to me in a dark and dizzying tunnel of confusion. I realized that quite possibly, what I had gone through in my life could very well have paralleled what my grandfather had gone through; if not in content, then at least in its interpretation. For my interpretation, initially, of what I was going through in my darkest days, was that of a person that was under some type of personal attack by an unknown force that would be very hard to describe, considering I wasn't even sure what the force was. I could relate to my grandfather when he mentioned in his letters that there were people and forces that were out to destroy him that many people did not know about.

However, as to what my grandfather's experience was, other than that, I could only imagine. I did know, though, that his mental illness eventually caused his ultimate demise. It apparently weighed heavily enough on him to cause him to stumble hard in life and never fully recover.

His brother's letter was a truly enlightened piece of spiritual inspiration meant to help my grandfather come to his senses, so as to say. But why didn't it work? At least it seemed like it had little effect on my grandfather, considering the negative path that my grandfather's life had taken in his later years. Why didn't my grandfather ask God for His help? Could it have been that he flat out didn't believe in God? But even if this were the case, how could my grandfather have lasted so many years without at least entertaining the idea that there is an all-powerful God, whose only intentions are good ones? Maybe his own personal demons had finally gotten the best of him. Maybe he truly wasn't interested in finding a different path to walk in life, other than the one that he was on.

I knew that my own personal path in life had become a very, very dark one after my demons had appeared to me. But were these demons real or something that my mind had created in an effort to somehow subordinate me to a darker force? Or quite possibly had my mind just created these scary sightings because I was ill in some way? Even though this letter contained some very pertinent information about spirituality as well as a wakeup call to my grandfather, it didn't seem to have any type of impact on him, spiritually or otherwise.

However, the same couldn't be said about my reaction to his letter. I had immediately found a connection to something higher in the letter; something that was very spiritual and profound. Quite possibly then, I was walking down a different path than my grandfather had walked- at least at this point in my life. Maybe I had taken a detour during a very critical point in my dark spiritual journey by asking God for His help and acknowledging that I would not survive without God's help. Or maybe I was just plain delusional, thinking that everything that had happened to me was purely spiritual in nature, when in fact it was the result of a mental illness that I had not been aware of.

But there was one thing that was quite possibly a thread that linked me to the spiritual world that lingered in my mind like an arrow that was waiting to be shot…the number 444.

A REALITY CHECK

It was in 1998 when I discovered a book called "The Messengers", written by G.W. Hardin and Julia Ingram, that I began to really gain some insight into the number 444. The book was about a man who apparently had many visitations by his angels and was led to disclose his previous life, in a different lifetime, as Paul the Apostle, in the bible. And it was also about the number 444 and how it had affected his life. His story transpired over two millennia and was now focused on his plan to reinstitute spirituality as it was known around two thousand years ago, now living as a modern day business man in Portland, Oregon.

Before "The Messengers" had been written, I had originally thought that the number 444 was somehow related to catastrophic events, although it is also true that some very enlightening and fantastic things happened when the number 444 had entered into my life. There was an initial sense of confusion when I first started seeing this number over seven years before "The Messengers" had been published and although I didn't know what the number meant, I did know that it carried some type of meaning.

During the seven years that I had been seeing this number, I was impressed by its ability to enter into my life in a myriad of ways and during some very crucial periods of time when I was gaining a sense of wonder about this number. I thought maybe it was related to the end of the world. I also thought that it was perhaps evil in its nature. I always appreciated it, though, when a fantastic event occurred in my life that was preceded by a "444 sighting". This gave me hope that this number was indeed related to something that was very good and it made me feel good about the possibility that good things were going to happen to me.

But when I finally bought a copy of "The Messengers" and read it, I began to realize that I was in over my head, as far as what it was that I was dealing with. This is when many crazy things started to happen in my life and also when I began to see things that were just "not normal". Demons, dreams, fears, spiritual warfare, alien nightmares, wars and even angry people that I did not even know, all seemed to creep into my life and hijack the peace that I had once known.

It is true that some wonderful things had happened to me during this period of time as well, but I sensed that they were somehow disconnected to what was going on in my life on another level. Even though I saw and heard the number 444 right before the birth of my first daughter, it did not seem as though she was at all related to any of the crazy things that were going on in my life at the time of her birth. In fact, it seemed rather as though she was the one who was going to save me from the hell that I was going through at the time, with her unconditional love.

There were monthly newsletters that were sent out by "The Messengers" organization to people who chose to subscribe to them, and I was one of them. The newsletters seemed to have a decidedly spiritual slant to them and brought up spiritual issues that were very pertinent to subjects like angels, demons, dreams, past lives, "444 sightings", and other subjects as well. They talked about people's relationship with Jesus and God and also their relationship to their angels. It all seemed very interesting and relevant, even though my dark period at this time seemed to get exponentially darker.

But what did other people think about their experiences with the number 444? Were people who were seeing this number having a wonderful time with their spiritual journey in life, or were they too beginning to see some very dark and evil things come into their life? It was too early on in the life of the internet to really consider "going online" to gain any type of information about this number in 1998 and the only thing that would appear during a search of this number, during this time, was related to "The Messengers."

But over a decade later it was obvious that some people were trying to connect with this number through internet websites dedicated to it, as well as forums that highlighted this number. It was fascinating to me to read the accounts on the internet from various people around the world who were currently trying to figure out the meaning of this number in their lives and why it kept occurring to them.

Some of these people's accounts were filled with questions and wonder, while others were filled with possible answers to the meaning of this number. Still other people were reporting some very strange events that were happening to them that were similar to what I had experienced during my "dark night of the soul." This was very interesting to me because it immediately dispelled the notion that the very dark things that I had seen were formed by a mind that was mad.

It also led me to believe that many people around

the world were beginning to see the number 444 and were beginning to wonder what it truly meant to them. I was finally able to connect to some people that were having a "444 experience" like the one that I had had. And I was beginning to see how my experience with this number was not an isolated one. During the time when "The Messengers" had been released, and for about a decade after that, I had not had the ability to figure out just how many people were seeing this number. Was it a few hundred or possibly a few thousand? And even as of the writing of this book, I was not sure how many people were beginning to see this number in their lives. I was intrigued, though, with the idea that there could be thousands of other people who were trying to figure out what this number meant in their life.

And while I have been trying to figure out why some very dark things had crept into my life while I was seeing this number, it's very interesting to me to note, though, that the only true salvation that came into my life, besides my daughter's unconditional love, was through another book that had to do with Jesus, as well. But it was of an entirely different ilk. And it was the way in which I discovered it that was very interesting to me.

THE LIGHT

It happened one day when I least expected. I was sitting down in a chair, thinking about all of the things that had happened to me recently while in my state of confusion and darkness. I remember I was thinking about a passage that I had read in my daily prayer book that was about "a place" that was being prepared for each and every one of us in this world by God. I was also thinking about some of the good things that had happened to me in my life, when all of a sudden I was overtaken by the most incredible feeling I had ever had in my life.

This feeling was accompanied by a strange but wonderful sensation. It was as if a very powerful light had emerged from behind my consciousness and slowly moved around my mind until it reached that point in my thought that was responsible for interpreting what I saw with my eyes in this world. This is the only way I know how to describe this feeling and it seemed to last for a minute or so. But within this short period of time I not only felt like I was being blinded by some type of brilliant light within my mind, but I was able to understand some incredible insights that seemed to be downloaded right into my mind by this powerful source of light.

I immediately understood how much God loves me and how much He loves every one of His children in this world. I could feel His unconditional love for every soul that was currently residing in this world. Even for people whom I would have questioned as being "good enough" for God's love. At this moment I began to realize that God loves each and every person in this world just as much as the next person. I realized that God not only loves who each and every person in this world is, but He also loves the potential that each person has in order to become the best person that they can in this world. This struck me as being incredible, considering that many people have passed through this world that have been fairly destructive or hateful people. I thought of all of the wars that had been created by individuals or governments that most people would think were evil and the murderous acts of yet others. But the insight that crashed through my mind ran counter to the idea that God hates anyone. In fact I realized that God only loves His children, even if they are destructive or hateful or unloving, themselves. According to my insight, apparently God realizes that even though some people in this world are not in line with His principles and are not aligning themselves with His will, He still loves them for many reasons. I realized that God truly does have an eternity to wait for people to come home to Him, no matter how much personal pain or suffering they may have to endure in order to be able to reconnect with Him. We have an infinite number of lives that we can live in this world and other worlds, and we can experience many things along the way that would move us in His direction.

Another insight flashed through my mind during this experience that left me with an incredible sense of awe at the power that God has. I realized that, in essence, God is really the only power in the universe, considering that He is the universe, and more. It was actually through a silly analogy that I realized this. The image of an atomic bomb crossed through my mind and at the same time I had the feeling of God's power and how insignificant an atomic bomb is compared to God's power. It is very easy to be impressed by the energy that an atomic bomb emits as it explodes, but this paled in comparison to the powerful energy that I was experiencing in this state of incredible discovery that I was going through. I felt completely at ease with the thought of nuclear weaponry in this world after this experience; because God is truly the only power in the universe.

I also saw, or comprehended a beach during this quick moment that I was in "the light" and realized that I am truly just a grain of sand on a beach that is universal in its size and scope. This would ordinarily have left me in a state of disbelief that my life was somehow unimportant to God and that I was just a grain of sand on a beach that stretched into infinity. But at the same time as this realization went through my mind I realized how humbling this insight was to me, but in a good way. I realized that God's love for me was tremendous, in its power and in its longevity; basically forever. And this made me realize that no matter how significant I thought my fears were, whether they were about nuclear war or death or other things, God is in control of my life and everyone else's in this world. It's just that we don't realize this most, or in some cases, all of the time.

I realized one more thing during this spiritually blinding moment; that this power, or light, had been with me for my entire existence; not just in this world, but for all eternity. It was as if this incredible power crept from behind my soul and into my mind to let me know, just for a moment, that I was being loved and protected, even through the most terrifying of times. Even though I had never before experienced this sense of power, accompanied by a spiritual light, I realized that it had always been there for me and would always be there for me eternally. And even though I never personally identified the source of this powerful light, I am sure that I was being given a glimpse of God's powerful light that we will all be going into eventually. There was no voice saying, "I am God"; just the most powerful feeling I have ever felt in my life, accompanied by a few very positive insights that I will never forget. This experience truly enlightened me to the fact that we all have a personal relationship with God that may not necessarily be based on conversations with God, but rather His undying love and support and protection for us, even in the worst of times. Even if we fail ourselves throughout our lifetime here on earth, God will never fail us. And even if we think that God's plan is not helping us currently in this lifetime, we must remember that God's plan for each and every one of us extends well beyond this lifetime into eternity.

THE LETTER

The following are excerpts from a letter that was written to my Grandfather by his brother. "…Year after year passed, you were always on a pedestal to me intellectually, socially, domestically. I know of your struggle with the practical…life you should have been living. But I never feared, I knew the years would awaken you to your responsibilities to God and to your soul. The dream I had of you was slowly unfolding, I had always hoped to awaken to a wonderful reality.

But what happened, Bud? All I know is from hearsay; things that came via the grapevine. And really I was hurt; hurt to the extent that I could say nothing because I did not want to admit to myself that you had failed me. I was hurt because I could feel. Hurt is the price we all pay for feeling. And pain is not accident, nor punishment, nor mockery, but it is a part of growth; the more we grow the more we feel, and the more we feel the more we suffer. For, if we are able to feel beauty, thrill and throb at it, we must also feel the lack of it. Those who glimpse heaven are bound to sight hell...I want you always to know Bud, that I think you are someone who can still be a great success. But you are as tall of soul, as strong of mind, and as reliable of heart as you feel you are in yourself. Money will not make you taller, power and prestige cannot help you; you are molded in the image of your Master and in that image you must dwell. Otherwise you must continue to walk around like a ghost. Lots of people are like that. They hang on a cross they cannot see…

Living the way you are, Bud, is an offense against the first law of life: 'Don't dry up!' All life began in the water. All bodies are composed largely of water. Water is essential for life. If the body loses its connection with water, it'll die. So, 'don't dry up' is still a fundamental law of life. And the law of the body is also the law of the spirit. That's the [strange] thing about physical law- it is tied so closely to mental and spiritual law. Minds must drink as well as bodies. Minds must be doused every so often in the common ocean of human experience or they dry up, become empty shells deprived of the pearl of self-respect. That's why wealth and success are greater risks for human beings than hardships and obscurity. That's why too much happiness and security are disastrous. They shut us away from the common experience. They make us think we're self-sustaining. And no one of us is. We need the stinging salt tides of troubles and responsibility to give us backbone. We need the dark floods of adversity and the fierce battering of the waves of competition to give us tolerance and humor, spunk and balance.

We have to jostle against all other fish to see how UNIMPORTANT we are. Bodies cannot endure on lonely mountain tops where no rain comes, nor in parched deserts. Neither can our minds flourish on mountain-peaks of selfishness, conceit, and foolish pride. We cannot live for ourselves alone, no matter how exquisite our culture may be or how lofty our standards. We must suffer and bear common experience- renew our life in the sea. Your sea is home- home with your wife, with your children, and with them alone- no matter the hardship, the suffering, you alone must prove your worth, your nobility of mind and heart and soul. Go back home, Bud, and live where the tides go in and out and open your heart to those tides.

I know you have your doubts and anger and fears, maybe rightly so, Bud. Yet far within you there is a place of peace. Deep in your soul is a refuge which fear cannot invade, nor horror defile. For, there is something in you stronger than fear, there is a spark of God in you that will survive all nightmares and that cannot be defeated or destroyed. And there is ONE within you whose strength and loyalty will never fail you. You have not seen His face nor heard His voice, and yet you can feel His presence like a living flame. And as long as He lives, you live- for you are a part of Him. No matter how demoralizing the things of life may be, know that your Father in heaven, your Creator of love, will walk with you to the very end of the trail…and the hills of His truth and beauty will shine forever above the dust and tears of lowly living…

So…forget the things that drained your courage, left you twisted in heart, robbed of faith. Forget the shabby bargains you made, the sordid dealings from others that betrayed your fresh ideals; forget them all and know that, with each day, you start again. Each night can end the blunders we all make, and each dawn can see the brave and honest battler, that we all long to be. We fail, we sin, but this alone is sure- your deep bright dreams of beauty [and] success shall go on. I pray [to] God in my daily mass to release your clinging to the litter of broken dreams and old mistakes and tattered shreds of tear-stained memories. I beg Him to give you strength to go with life where it left off, using the ashes of your yesterdays to feed and cradle the new glory of today."

GOD CALLING

God was calling me, but was I listening? It happened one day while I was in the throes of my spiritual crisis. I remember I was working as a flight attendant on an airplane that was being boarded by passengers. There was a woman who had boarded early and had sat down towards the back of the airplane where I was working. This woman seemed to have a sense of peace and grace that I had not seen in people very often. I tried not to stare at her although I wondered what truly made her seem to be of a grace not known to me. It was when I was walking past her that I noticed she was holding a book up in front of her. There was the title in bold letters; "God Calling." I immediately knew that I should get this book as soon as possible because of the almost otherworldly sense of peace that this woman had about her and the effect that this book had possibly had on her ability to practice this peace. And while this is probably the most difficult thing to explain, it must have been my angels that were directing my attention to her and the book that she was reading.

I almost couldn't wait to get to my layover so that I could buy this book and find out what it was about. Perhaps under normal circumstances I may have asked this woman what the book was about and where she had bought it. But because I was working as a flight attendant for a major airline, I was required to respect the passengers on board in a professional manner. So I assumed a professional demeanor and decided to explore this book on my own.

When I got to the city that I was laying over in, I immediately went out to a bookstore that was in town and found "God Calling". I discovered that it was written by two authors referred to as "The Two Listeners" and was edited by a person known as A.J. Russell. The book was about two people who had apparently been visited by Jesus, or the spirit of Jesus and were subsequently given a message by Jesus for every day of the year. These messages were of a spiritual nature and contained many things that were like answers to the spiritual problems that I was facing during my spiritual crisis. The power of these daily messages was so great to me that I found myself, at first, reading an occasional daily message. By this I mean that I was learning about spirituality in a very deep way and it was almost impossible, at first, to read a message a day, as the book was designed for. This was because I was not yet accustomed to receiving the depth of information that each daily message contained while trying to assimilate the message on a spiritual level every day.

However, I soon discovered that what the book had to relate to me was of a very powerful origin and seemed to be making more sense to me than any other source of spiritual information that I had recently been exposed to. In fact the truth would be that this book would remain as the single most important source of spirituality to me for years to come. Even as my spiritual crisis seemed to diminish in its intensity over time, I still relied on this book to buoy me above the worldly days that many times brought me stress and anguish and seemed to wear me out. I began to realize that this book was a true source of spiritual inspiration for me and the pages of this book really seemed to "talk" to me through the years.

How lucky I felt that this book had entered into my life through my brief encounter with the woman who seemed to me to transcend this world. But luck really had nothing to do with it, as I would realize later on in my life. The fact that I had been engaged with several different sources of spiritual information during my spiritual crisis that had presented the power of Jesus and his teachings in this world seemed to represent some type of synchronicity that simply could not be ignored. "God Calling", however, ultimately represented to me, over time, the one source that was truly directly linked to Jesus and ultimately represented what was to become my only source of salvation. With that being said, I also obviously resorted to the Bible many times during my spiritual crisis. But "God Calling" would still remain the most read book for me during my "dark night".

It was through this book that I would discover the meaning of many of Jesus' teachings. Even though this book offered many messages that I had never heard of before, they were all laced with spirituality and became a part of my daily spiritual ritual that eventually offered me enough insight into the spiritual world that I was able to free myself from the bonds of my spiritual crisis by realizing that I was a true child of God who could embrace God's special gifts of Love, Joy, Protection, Life, Power and Truth, as well as many others. Once I opened my door to Jesus and God I began to realize that I had been enslaved by a force that was bent on destroying the peace that I had once had in my life. I also realized that no person or power would ever again be able to take my peace and joy from me, as long as I remained true to Jesus and God through what I had learned from my spiritual crisis, and especially from the book "God

Calling."

HEALING PATHS

God is fantastic! There is nothing He can't do when it comes to turning our lives around. He views us as His children and He knows that it is inevitable that we will get into a little trouble in this life due to the free will that He has given us. This free will allows us to do things in life as we see fit to do them. Without this free will we might be bound completely to His way of doing things or maybe we would not be able to do as many things as we would otherwise choose to do. On the one hand, this free will that we have literally frees us to try different things in life that we might not otherwise do if we were still following God's will. But this is the way this life was designed for us and this is what God had in mind when He designed this world. He knows that we are going to make mistakes and this is O.K. with Him. He understands that we might not take the straight and narrow path in life.

If we follow His commandments or way of living in life, our life might seem to become boring or mundane to us. We might feel that our style is being cramped or that our way of living is being stifled. But the fact that we could possibly feel this way is fine with God. He knows that until we discover the things that we need to discover in this life we may not be ready to accept His will or His way of living. He would never want to get in our way and although He is always ready to show us His will or way of living, He will never stop us from doing the things that we want to do in this life. The only exception to this would be if an individual is ready to accept God's will in everything that they do. When an individual decides to accept God's will completely in their life, then some pretty amazing things can happen.

When we accept God's will it could seem at first that God has an entirely different plan for us than the plan that we would choose for ourselves in life. By this it is meant that accepting God's will involves many things that we must get used to. When we accept His will we also accept the direction that He has for us. His direction may be entirely different than the direction that we would take ourselves in on a daily basis. But when we accept the direction that He has for us in life then we can also accept many other things, like His protection. One way that God protects us is by preventing us from doing some things in life that would not be good for us. He is unlimited in the ways that He can do this.

For example, we may decide to do something in life and then proceed with our plans to do this thing. But our plans may soon become derailed or completely sidetracked. This may very well be due to God's protection that He has for us. When our plans don't work out in life as we had expected them to, we can either become absolutely frustrated or we can choose to believe that God had some intervention in our life that helped to change our plans. Why would God choose to change our plans in life that we sometimes work so hard to complete? It is because He is protecting us. There are many things in this life that can be very hurtful to people and God is only protecting us when He helps us down another path in life other than the one we sometimes find ourselves on.

Even our plans that involve the greatest of intentions can sometimes create a completely different outcome than we expected if these plans are allowed to be carried out according to our will. And many times this could involve a negative outcome. But we can't see the future, nor can we see the eventual outcome of our plans in life. Only God knows what the eventual outcome of our plans will be and this is why He actively blocks our plans from time to time with a "spiritual stop sign". This can be very frustrating to people and rightfully so because of the anger and frustration that results from their plans being cancelled.

However, if we choose to look at the end result a little differently, then not only will we feel better about our plans in life being changed, but we can also accept what God has in store for us. He may very well have a different plan for us than what we thought would be the best plan. If we can learn to accept this seemingly very difficult process then we can begin to accept the gifts that God has for us. This process can become very simple over time when it is put into practice in someone's life. There may always seem to be an initial feeling of frustration when our plans seem to fall apart. But if we can immediately choose to accept God's different plan for us and then also thank God for the plan that He has for us we can rest assured that we are going to be in much "calmer waters" than if we had forged ahead with our own plans. We can all remember a time in life when we were able to complete our plans and the result was anything from disappointment to complete catastrophe.

There are different forces at work in our world and when we choose to forge ahead with our own plans in life instead of praying to God for His direction, we are often times allowing other forces to enter into our life and take control of our plans. These other forces may not have the best of intentions when it comes to completing our plans for us. We may find that the plans we had originally made somehow become something that could potentially harm us in life; either in the way that the plans unfold or with the final negative result of these plans. It is not that the plans that we have in life are bad plans. It is just that our plans can many times be compromised by other forces that are not completely in line with God's will. When this happens we often times wish we had never planned to do what we ended up doing. How many times have we said to ourselves, "I wish I had never done that."

If we align ourselves with God's will and pray to Him for His direction, then we will never have to utter those words again- hopefully. By aligning ourselves with God we will still have to learn our lessons in life, but they will be learned in the safety of God's will. It may be that the severity of these lessons that we still need to learn in life will be blunted by the many things that God offers us in order to make our life here in this world a little easier, and in many cases a lot easier.

For example, He offers us His forgiveness for things that we have done in life that we later wish we had not done. By accepting His forgiveness we can continue on with our lives and be free from any guilt that we may have had from doing something that we should not have done. But we must also make sure that we never do the things again that we have been forgiven of by God. It is like Jesus said, "You are forgiven. Now go forward and sin no more." If we find that this is not possible than we must be prepared for the fact that the plans we make in life may continue to be influenced in a negative way by other forces that are not aligned with God. We will continue to have to learn our lessons in life the hard way.

Another way that God loves to help us in this life is by offering us His healing power. There is no limit to the amount of ways that God can heal us. Whether it is physically, mentally, spiritually or in some other way, He is not limited in the ways that He can heal us. His healing power is just waiting to come into our lives. But we must be ready for this power to enter into our lives in order to receive the healing that He has for us. We must first accept His will, and then accept the fact that He will show us a different way of living. It's true, when we accept His will our lives may begin to change rapidly. So how do we become ready for His healing power?

Many people are naturally ready to receive His healing power in their lives. This may be due to the fact that they have had a very difficult life in some way and are very ready to change that part of their life. When someone's life has been very difficult for them for a long time, they may wish very deeply that their life was changed in a positive way forever. This is when God can enter into our being and deliver His mighty healing power. And it is always up to God to decide when the time is right for His healing power to enter into someone's life. A person may wonder for years if they will ever be healed by God or if it is even possible to be healed by God. But God will enter into a person's life at just the right time. We are constantly learning the things that we need to learn in this life whether through hardship or enlightenment. One of the most difficult things to learn is that it is always up to God as to when He will reward us with His healing power.

Sometimes we feel that we can no longer continue on in this life with the ailment or the problems that we have in life. We feel that we could just as easily not continue on with this life or we feel that we will never be able to get out of the negative situations that we sometimes find ourselves in. But God understands many things about us that we don't understand about ourselves. He understands just how much we can handle in this life. He understands at what point we can truly no longer go on living. So he watches us carefully and He listens to us closely when we pray to Him, but it is He who decides just when it is that we receive His wonderful gift of healing. And while it may seem at times that His healing can't come soon enough, God's timing in our lives is always perfect.

His healing can come in many ways. It could come in the form of a wonderful change in our life. Whether this is a job promotion, a long awaited move to another home or city, or another wonderful thing that would change our situation in life in a positive way. It could also come in the form of a physical healing that we never realized could happen through God's wonderful healing energy. There is truly no limit to the power of God's healing. We only need to pray to Him earnestly and then thank Him in advance for His wonderful healing to take place in our lives, if we are truly ready to receive His healing power.

There is also no end to the way in which He can deliver His wonderful healing power. He is never limited in the way in which His healings arrive in our lives. The one thing we must always remember to do, though, is thank Him in advance of His healing that He has for us. This shows Him that we have faith in Him and that we also truly appreciate His healing power. When we thank Him, it is like we have opened our spiritual door to Him. It is like we are saying to Him, "I love you God and I truly wish to accept Your healing power into my life",

He can also heal us spiritually. Some people may wonder what this means exactly. There is an entirely different world in front of us that we cannot see very well, if at all. This world is the spiritual world and it is actually completely intertwined within the material world in which we live. It is distinctly different than our world, yet completely operative in our world. How can this be? It is because the spiritual world is unseen by most people in this world. It is something that our physical senses can not readily identify with. Because of this, most of us assume that there is no spiritual world at play in our physical world and that we will only experience this spiritual world after we have passed from this world. But it is entirely true that the spiritual world is right here with us, right now.

When God offers us spiritual healing, He is offering His world to us. This is a very wonderful thing! Many of us don't realize that our soul, spirit and mind reside in an entirely different place than in this material world. Yet our soul, spirit and mind are integrated into this material world in a way that is very hard to understand. And just like in this physical world, there are other negative forces at work in the spiritual world that can directly affect our soul, spirit and mind. We may not be able to understand these negative spiritual forces that are at work, but they have a direct influence on what happens to us in our everyday experience here in this world. This is why God's spiritual healing power is so important to us on a spiritual level. He has the power to eliminate all negative spiritual forces that would seem to affect us or potentially harm us in this life. A spiritual healing may very well be the most important thing that we could ever receive from God, because this type of healing has a directly positive effect on our soul, spirit and mind. This in turn has a direct positive effect on our lives in this world.

When our soul, spirit and mind are all aligned with God, then we are truly under the power of God's protection and we can expect our lives to become infinitely better because of this. His spiritual healing power can align our spiritual life so that we are not influenced by anything other than His beautiful will. God's will is something that we should never take for granted in this life. Even if we feel the need to stray from God or possibly try something that we know is not right in life, we should resist this temptation and instead pray to God for His strength and courage to carry on in life. And even when we feel we cannot carry on in life, just pray to God and rest assured that He is in control of our lives. But we must pray to God for His will and also constantly thank God for all of the good things that He has given to us in this life. This will enable us to accept His wonderful gift of healing that He has for us.

However, healings may sometimes take months or years until we receive them from God. It is not that He wants us to wait that long for the healing that He has for us, it is that we are not ready for the healing yet. It is possible that we have not yet learned what we need to learn from a difficult situation in life before we receive His healing. This is very hard for most people to understand. But God will provide the means and the time for the healing that He so desperately wishes to give us. Another difficult thing to realize about the spiritual world and our relationship with God is that many of us are not ready for what God has for us. This is because we have subconscious blocks within us that prevent us from gaining from God what He wants to give us. We may simply say to ourselves, "I don't believe in God", or "God doesn't want to help me". These are subconscious beliefs that we have and they are engrained in our daily life. These types of beliefs, or blocks, do not allow us to accept what God already wants to give us.

We may also simply believe that God can not heal us or that He will not heal us. We need to have more faith in God in order to accept His healing that He has for us. Gaining more faith in God can be a long process, though, in and of itself. It can take years for a person to realize that God truly does want to help them and that there is nothing that God cannot do in a person's life. It may be that a person who has little faith in God must experience a "difficult period" in life that finally causes them to turn to God for His help. The stronger a person's belief is that God does not want to help them, then quite possibly the tougher the time that person may have in life before they ask God for His help. It is during the toughest of times in life when we may finally resort to asking God for His help. Whether it is in the trenches of war or in a battle with cancer, many of us may need to experience something in life that we know we may not overcome without the help of a greater power-God.

GOD'S HELP

Tough times in life come in all sorts of shapes and sizes. They could be a difficult financial situation or a disease that is unrelenting. Tough times can also happen on a spiritual level and can catch many of us unaware as to what is happening. The spiritual level, or spiritual world, is a place that not many of us are familiar with. It may seem that when the topic of spirituality is brought up by someone, we immediately assume that some type of religious conversation is going to follow. But spirituality is not bound by today's religions. Spirituality encompasses many things and is defined by many different beliefs. There are both good beliefs and bad beliefs about spirituality that can affect our lives directly. It is up to everyone to discover which beliefs are the best ones to believe in.

At first, our fears and anxieties may influence what we believe in spiritually. So may our habits in life. If we turn ourselves over to the many vices and bad habits that this world has to offer us, we may become weakened physically, mentally and ultimately, spiritually. It is then that our fears we may have about things may seem to take over and may lead us in a different spiritual direction than that of God. It has been said that all paths lead to God, and this is true. We can unknowingly take a very fearful spiritual path in life that initially leads us away from God. But how far we go down a fearful and negative spiritual path depends on many things. Among them are, our initial faith in God, the strength of our fears, the demons that we may have on a spiritual level, and other things as well. But even the mightiest oak tree can be felled. By this it is meant that even those of us who have a very powerful inclination to resist God can be spooked deeply enough, on a spiritual level, to eventually ask God for His help. All paths do lead to God.

So when a difficult spiritual period in life comes our way, it is always best to pray to God and ask Him for His help. It is true too, that God will answer our prayers in His own time. It may be best for some of us to receive His help immediately (this is always God's wish). However, it may be best for some people to go through a prolonged negative spiritual experience so that they can better understand who

God is, by literally understanding who, or what, God is not. This can only help a person to accept His healing in their lives. For when we truly know God, then we can truly accept His help and healing in our life. It may be that the strongest faith in God is borne of the toughest of times. Or that those of us who may have a very dark spiritual experience in life can learn about what God is not. By learning about what God is not, we can learn about what God is. Simply put, we can learn about the light by learning about the darkness first.

This may be one of the toughest ways to learn about God, but it is certainly a way in which an enduring faith can be planted into the soul of someone who may never have, otherwise, believed in God. Why is it important to believe in God? So that He may deliver His help and His healing to us. It is the negative spiritual beliefs that we may have that prevent us from accepting all the good things that God has in store for us. And it is not only God's healing that is important for us in life, but also all of the other things that God has for us that we know nothing about- all of the things that we take for granted on any given day.

Some of the things that God gives us are His Love and His Joy. He also provides us with His Compassion and His Protection. If we have faith in God, then He also strengthens our faith in Him so that any obstacles that may come our way in life can be removed by God, and in His own way. All these things are the most important things that we could possibly receive on a daily basis. God's Love knows no boundaries and it can come into our lives in an infinite number of ways. It can be the smile that we see on a little child's face, or it can be the companionship that a friend or even a special pet can offer to us. His Love can enter our lives on a daily basis and provide the kind of feelings that we need in life in order to continue on with our lives.

His Joy is another beautiful thing that He gives to us. It is something that makes us feel very good and that can make us laugh when something unexpectedly funny happens. His Joy can erase negative emotions that we harbor on a spiritual level. It can also turn a devastatingly gloomy day into one of the best days ever. This can happen at any time and many of us take it for granted that God is helping us on a daily basis. That is why it is always so important to thank God for all of the good things that He has given to us and also for all of the good things that He will be giving to us in the future. It is important to remember that the good things that He gives us are not always material in nature and are more often of a spiritual nature, like His Love and His Joy. And we need look no further than to God's powerful Protection in our lives to understand how important God is in our daily life.

For those of us who have had a dark spiritual experience in life, or are going through one now, it is especially important to understand that God will protect us from all things evil. God has the power to eliminate the negative spiritual forces that can seem to invade our lives from time to time. It is only when we seem to stray from God, whether knowingly or unknowingly, that our lives can take a turn for the worse. Sometimes it may only be a warning of a spiritual nature that we receive that can put us back on the right path. But sometimes it may be more than a warning that comes into our lives and we get back into spiritual trouble. These are the times that we need to come back to God and pray to Him for His Love and Protection. We also need to pray for a stronger faith in God so that we don't ever stray from Him again.

God understands that we are going to make mistakes in life, but it is when we decide to repeat these mistakes over and over again, that we get into spiritual trouble. It is true that sometimes we don't even know that we are doing something bad because we may not consider what we are doing to be a bad thing. Other times we may have a strong justification for doing something that we know is wrong and so we go ahead and do it anyway. This is when we can also fall into a negative spiritual path that can leave us in spiritual trouble again.

How do we know when we have fallen into a negative spiritual path? Sometimes it is hard to recognize or realize that we have done so. The signs that we are in trouble are unmistakable, but the way in which these signs are sometimes interpreted may lead us to believe that the path we are on is not a bad one. There are other negative forces at work in the spiritual world that would love to confuse us and have us believe that the path we are on is a good path, even though we may be on a more negative path. If we can accept that feelings of depression, confusion, fear, hopelessness, despair, anxiety, anger and other negative feelings, are not what God wants us to be feeling, than we can accept that we are generally headed down the wrong spiritual path in life if we are feeling these things. This is especially true if we are feeling these negative things on a regular basis. For God truly wants us to feel loved and feel full of hope in our life. He wants us to feel joyous and he wants us to have fun in life. He knows that we may run into problems from time to time, but overall He wants us to have a wonderful life.

If we should discover that we are on a path in life that is not the path that we want to be on, then we must take action to get onto a better path in life. The best thing we can do is to pray to God for His spiritual help. And while he chooses not to make us leave the spiritual path we are on, He may choose to leave us clues as to what type of path we are on and what type of decisions we need to make in order to get onto a better spiritual path. What kind of clues may God leave us? He may actually send us messages that could leave an impression on us. And how does He do this?

God is unlimited in the ways that He can communicate with us. Our dreams often times have messages in them that when reflected upon could give us a clue as to what we should be doing differently in our lives. Or at the very least our dreams can help us decide if we are on a good or bad path in life. Synchronicity is also very important when it comes to having clues given to us from God. Do we keep seeing the same word over and over in a short period of time? Or do we keep seeing the same subject pop up several times in a short period of time? These then may be clues as to what God wants us to pay attention to. Is there a message in this synchronicity? Should we possibly focus on what these messages mean that were sent to us through synchronicity by God? The answer is yes. If we sit down and really think about what messages are coming our way, then we might begin to understand what God wants us to do differently in our lives. Sometimes we can realize what the message is about very quickly. But other times it may take us months or years before we say to ourselves, "Got it."

When we finally "get it", or when we finally

understand the message, it is best to immediately put that message to work in our lives. We may receive messages about love, hatred, respect, humility, war, hope, work, ailments, friendships, anything really. When this happens it is time to think about the message and start wondering how we can incorporate this message into our lives in a positive way. Many times God has messages for us that we don't really want to hear. "Love more", "work harder", "rest more", "listen", "teach", "respect". We may ask ourselves, "How can I do more of this, or less of that?" These are questions that are asked during times of intense spiritual growth. And these may be the things that God would have us work on in our lives in order to get onto a better spiritual path.

There may also be times when very menacing messages come to us through our dreams, synchronicity or other means. God may not be the only one who is trying to reach you. Other negative forces in the spiritual realm may be trying to dominate you or frighten you or get your attention. This is when we have to pray as hard as we can to God and thank Him over and over again for His protection. Most of the time He will dispel these negative messages and the fear that they can carry with them. However, there are times when God may let us stay on our negative spiritual path for a while longer than we would like to. This is so that we can learn from our mistakes and possibly learn about our fears and negative beliefs that are helping to keep us on our negative spiritual path. But rest assured that the sooner we can learn from our negative spiritual path, the sooner we can get back onto a better spiritual path. And it is also very important to know that no matter how bad it might seem sometimes, God is always with you and wishing that you can hurry back home to your right spiritual place in life. But many times this is up to us. We may have to give up habits or vices or negative ways of thinking in order to "get back home." Many times we may have to give up something that brings us pleasure in life that may also be harming ourselves or others, and this is not always easy.

But if we can at least figure out what it is that we need to change in our lives, then we can make the decision to change. It has been said that life is full of decisions that we have to make. This is no more true than in our spiritual lives. Every day that we put off making the right spiritual decisions is a day spent on the wrong spiritual path. And while some of us may be able to remain on our negative spiritual paths and still enjoy our lives, others are beginning to experience the collision of this material world with the "unseen" spiritual world. They are beginning to realize that spiritual forces beyond their control and understanding are starting to influence their lives directly. It is almost as if the door to another dimension is being slowly opened so that they can see where they stand spiritually. After all, the spiritual world is where we are all going to after our life here in this world is over. So why not experience the spiritual world right now and get our "spiritual house" in order right now? Especially since God is helping us right now.

PRAYER OF THANKS

Thank you God for Your presence in our lives today and every day, for here and forever. We thank you for Your beautiful supply of Love, Peace, Truth, Hope, Mercy, Joy, Gratitude, Beauty, Faith, Courage and other things unspoken. Your Love so that all fear and anger are dispelled in our lives, giving us freedom from all things not created by You. Your Peace so that all anxiety in our lives is removed, giving us the tranquility that we so desire in times that are often trying. Your Truth so that all confusion in our lives is removed, creating crystal clarity in our minds so that we can understand Your will, Your plan for us. Your Hope so that all depression is removed from our lives, our faith renewed in You so that we can live our life with joy. Your Mercy so that we understand that it is not Your wish for us to suffer, nor is it Your wish for us to feel the shame that another would cast upon us. Your Joy so that we can enjoy our lives and we can shine Your light upon other souls that we meet in our daily life. Your Gratitude that You give to us so that we may return this sense of complete thankfulness to you, creating an unbreakable circle of trust and respect between us. Your Beauty so that we can fully appreciate Your creation across our universe and others, spreading Your wish for all things to express their greatest potential in this life and others. Your Faith so that all mountains can be removed, even by Your faintest breath, allowing us to move ever forward in our quest for eternal union with You. Your Courage so that we may defeat all negativity in our life and accept Your plan with an open heart and an open mind.

And we especially give thanks for all those things that we may take for granted that You give to us, do for us, and wish for us every moment of every day. And these are some things that we truly thank You for: our health when we have it; the food that You give to us when we eat; the friends that we have when we gather; the shelter that You give to us to rest in, whatever it may be; the strength that You give to us to make it through each day; the protection that You tirelessly give to us from all evil things; the gentleness that You grace us with when we need it the most; the unspoken power that You encompass us with every moment of every day; and all of the other things that

You give to us that we cannot even imagine living without, every moment of our lives, and that we may unknowingly take for granted.

Thank you God for being a just God whose principles are unbending, even in the face of the devil's confusion. Thank you God for being an all powerful God whose power is unmatched, even by the devil himself. Thank you God for being a merciful God who is always forgiving and always remindful when we stray, by gently pushing us in Your direction through Your graceful, eternal embrace. Thank you God for Your supply of only good things that we so often take for granted in our lives. Thank you God for never giving up on us, even in our moments of weakness, for always helping us and allowing us to come back to You. Thank you God for the eternity that You have spread out before us, so that we may return home to You in our own time; for not pushing us so hard that we break. Thank you for all of these things and more, from the bottom of our hearts and from the deepest part of our souls; that part that is connected to You. And should we ever find ourselves in a moment of weakness in our lives and may not be able to recite this prayer, or any other prayers to You, then please remember our moments when we have prayed to You in earnest; when we gave You our complete gratitude, when we promised You our own life to keep forever, when we pledged our own life to You, eternally. Thank you, God.

PART TWO

THE ELIJAH PROJECT: A

BOOK OF DREAMS

ELIJAH

Are you walking by…just walking by? Have you walked by that homeless person on the street again? Did you even look at them? Did you meet their gaze? Did you meet their request? Was it for money, or was it for food? Did you give them what they wanted, or did you just walk away?

Many of us would have walked away…end of story. But for those of us who have entertained an honest request for a second chance in life, another thing can happen. Help may be given where help is needed. Have you ever looked deep into someone's eyes and wondered why it is that they are willing to sacrifice their decency or sense of self respect in life in order to request a meager handout from someone they don't even know? How did they get to this point in life that they are actually asking a stranger for money? How did they get to the point that they are standing on a street corner, wondering where their next meal will come from?

I would say that there is more to the story than what most people would assume. I would say that you are potentially looking into the eyes of an angel who has fallen...who is here on your behalf. Yes, here for you. Many people may think that this couldn't be true, but I would remind them that the workings of the spiritual world are much different than that of the material world. And I would also remind them that many of the greatest prophets to have ever transited this world were as poor as anyone you have ever seen in this lifetime. And they were obviously seeking some type of reprieve from this world's harshest conditions when they sought out the shelter of a Good Samaritan; someone who would gladly help them in their struggle against something like starvation.

And so it might be for some of today's hungriest people...just why are they on the street corners and busy intersections begging for money, or food? Why have they become this desperate? Are they just drug addicts, or financial flunkies who have ignored consistent employment in life? What if they are Angels, starving on the corner of your street, just waiting for the opportunity to talk to you? What if they are truly the incarnation of an Angel's spirit into a human body? Would you just walk by them and judge them as possibly someone who had not worked hard enough in life to justify the end results of hard work, like food on the table, or shelter for themselves?

What if these people are truly Angels, waiting to be engaged? Would you risk the opportunity of walking by an Angel in disguise, instead of greeting them, and inviting what conversation may come from them, as desperate as someone would be who was in need of food? What if the conversation that you had with them would somehow put you on a different track, or path in life…a path that was more enlightened? Would you risk this chance for a few dollars? How about for a few hundred dollars? At what point would you walk away from serious spiritual change that could change the direction in which you were heading in this life? Especially if it determined what direction you might be heading into in the next life.

Legend has it that Elijah, the great prophet in the Bible, was at one point disguised as a beggar. And when he confronted a wealthy man, his request for this man was to observe the presence of God and to praise God in his daily activities. So, what if some of the poorest of people in this world were really Angels, or prophets in disguise, for that matter? What if the next person in this world that asked you for money was really the spirit of Elijah, disguised as a drug addict? What if he begged you for just one dollar to help him out in this world? Would you give it to him, or would you just walk by? What if he held the key to your next spiritual destination, and you just bypassed that opportunity by walking on?

These are questions that we need to ask ourselves now, as this world descends further into economic chaos. What are we going to do when confronted with the opportunity to help someone else in this world that is not doing as well as we are? Are we going to just walk on past them, or are we going to embrace the possibility that this is perhaps the spirit of Elijah, himself, that is asking us for our help and is willing to give us his help in *return? The choice is yours...to become involved in the daily workings of our current economic disaster, or run from it by just ignoring the pleas of someone who may have the fate of their family members, and possibly your spiritual future, riding on your decision to give, or not to give. So think deeply, even when it comes to giving just a little...will I engage, perhaps even in a new spiritual direction, or will I just walk away?*

ANOTHER DAY

There he was, on the other side of the street, waving at me with the confidence and swagger that only someone whom I would have known for twenty years or more could have done. He smiled confidently at me, with a cigarette in his mouth. Although he was unshaven, he wore what seemed to be a brand new, gray colored suit, complete with black leather shoes. His combed back, charcoal gray hair, matched his attire and added a sense of confidence and wisdom to his demeanor. I saw that he was saying something to me that seemed to be very important to him, but I couldn't understand him; the traffic that crawled between us muffled out his attempt at communicating with me.

However, as I kept walking down my side of the sidewalk that I was on, I looked intently into his eyes and only recognized someone that I did not know. I realized that I had never made the acquaintance of this man, nor had I ever seen him before. But my first thought was to wave back. If this man seemed so comfortable as to flag me down from across the street and even smile at me confidently as he did, then I must have met him at some point in my life. Maybe I just couldn't remember who this man was; maybe he did know me, but I was the one who was misplacing the familiarity that I would have had with someone like him.

I chose to walk on and acknowledge his greeting as one that would have been aimed at someone else that had been in my vicinity, someone that I had not seen, but was the intended recipient of his salutation. So I made my way into the coffee shop that I was walking to by transitioning the few extra steps down the sidewalk and through the entrance, into the familiar shop that smelled of lattes and freshly toasted bagels. I ordered a small Americano and during the few moments that it took for the barista to prepare my drink, I looked across the shop and through the window that offered a view out into the cityscape of the small Rhode Island town that I had recently moved to. I noticed the same buildings that the man who had waved at me was standing in front of. There was the small art shop, the barber shop that had been there for over fifty years and a brand new boutique pet supply shop that had only recently opened. But there was no sign of the man that had waved at me. Where had he gone? Was he really just a business man, or perhaps a stock broker that had wanted to tell me something important? Or was he just waving at someone else that I had not seen?

My attention turned back to the woman behind the counter who was offering me the drink that I had ordered. I gave her the money that was due and moved out through the coffee shop's entrance onto the sidewalk that housed several outdoor tables, complete with chairs and "no smoking" signs. No smoking, I thought to myself. I remembered the time in my life that I had regularly smoked some of the strongest cigarettes that had been available to me at the time. At one point I was even rolling my own, unfiltered, so as to enjoy the strongest smoke available. It had been over twenty years since I had engaged in this risky habit, but even the mention of smoking at this point in my life brought back memories of my long forgotten habit. I also thought how the man I had seen across the street was smoking a cigarette. No coffee for him at these tables, I thought to myself. The irony of this last thought would last in my mind for quite some time as the owner of this particular coffee shop walked out onto the sidewalk and over to my table to make sure that the newly attached "no smoking" sign would stay fixed to the table top that my coffee was resting on.

I engaged her in a short, but enlightening conversation, that revolved around the need for these newly placed "no smoking" signs, recently put upon each table top. Apparently they were placed there to help ward off the early afternoon patrons that frequented this coffee shop on warm afternoons. The exact crowd that the coffee shop owner was referring to was a group of people that would sit at these tables after they had ordered a small cup of coffee that would be nursed through the rest of the afternoon with plenty of cigarettes, as well. The smoke from these cigarettes would inevitably make its way into the coffee shop and create an unwanted atmosphere within. In an effort to dismantle this fairly frequent occurrence, the owner had placed "no smoking" signs on the tops of the tables that stood upon the sidewalk.

It wasn't the fact that the owner had fully explained the habits of the crowd that inhabited these tables during the afternoon that really surprised me, it was the fact that I had also learned from the owner that there was a methadone clinic nearby that harbored this particular crowd in the morning hours before they would occupy these tables in the afternoon. The owner didn't mention who they were or what they looked like, but she did convey that they were more of a nuisance, with their smoking, than anything else.

Very interesting, I thought to myself.

Methadone…heroine…the two were inseparable…at least to someone who was trying to kick a habit such as heroine. This was something that kept running through my mind as I pictured the gentleman on the other side of the street that had been waving at me, as if he had known me forever. I wondered if this man was one of the people who had frequented this shop, maybe even this very table that I was seated at, on a regular basis. How funny it was to me then, that our acquaintance had perhaps only been cut off by a matter of hours, instead of a matter of heavily trafficked feet. In other words, perhaps I had not already met this man, not because I hadn't returned his friendly wave and crossed the street to shake his hand, but because our schedules were just a few hours off, on a daily basis. I would attend this coffee shop in the morning, and he would stop by in the afternoon, assuming of course that he was even a part of the afternoon coffee shop crowd that chain smoked their cigarettes and let the effects of their newly introduced methadone rule their world.

I couldn't help but think how this man had almost seemed like someone I had known from the past, but couldn't fully recognize. As I stood up from the chair that had been supporting me for the past forty-five minutes, I wondered if I would ever see that man again, considering he was now not welcome at the tables that comprised a regular part of my routine when I was not working. I wondered if I would ever see him again walking down the sidewalk. And as to why I was even fixated on this very thing was beyond my comprehension. I would just have to wait and see what fate had in store for me.

MONEY

It may seem as though our life may never come to the point that we all wish it would come to- the point at which we are all satisfied with where we are in our life. Do we have enough money? Do we have enough food? Do we have the shelter that we dream of? Are we completely satisfied with how our life is? And how about what we think is owed to us, either by this world, or by a higher power? What do these things have to do with our current situation in life and how does this relate to our complete satisfaction in life?

It may also seem as though our satisfaction in life is based on the acquisition of material goods and perhaps even services in our life. But maybe the truth is further from this line of thinking than most people are willing to admit to. How many people have you read about that are completely unsatisfied with their lives, even though they command the ebb and flow of their very finances in life? Do you think, even for a moment, that their lives are comforted by the millions of dollars that they may have at their command? The sad truth to this answer, is no. No matter how many millions of dollars an individual may accumulate in this lifetime, their ultimate happiness is not dependent on their wealth, but rather their relationship with God.

Do you think that this is not true? Than just think of your most unhappy moments in life...think hard...You will see that at those moments your happiness was not ruled by the amount of money in your bank account, but rather by the complete joy that ruled your life, or rather the amount of joy that was absent in your life. God's Joy is the greatest equalizer there is. Either you have it, or you don't. It doesn't matter what your bank account statement says, you are either joyous, or you are not. This is a stark realization that many people must endure in order to become truly happy in life. We only need to look at one of the most poignant figures in life as far as joy is concerned, to realize that our joy is not related to how much money we command at any moment. And who was this figure that we are talking about; none other than Jesus, himself.

He had the ability to completely rule his local environment with the kind of joy that is only known on a higher level. He could keep an entire company of people in a state of laughter and joy that only God, Himself, could deliver. Believe it or not, but Jesus was able to induce such a state of joy and laughter that all people in his presence would feel completely at ease with life and also with their own troubles in life. He was able to transform even a hard core believer in hardship and trouble into a person that had only high hopes in life. But what does this mean for people who are in this life right now, somehow disconnected from Jesus' time? Do they have any chance at all of reaping the benefits of Jesus' magnificent ability to transform trouble into carefree laughter?

Just believe…believe. Because faith in Jesus, and God, our Father, is all anyone needs in this life to completely benefit from that "greater power's" joyous influence on our life. If this seems too simple for any person to believe in, than just try the opposite…tell yourself that there is no hope in this world for you to ever feel joyous or happy. Just tell yourself that there is no chance that you will ever be happy again in this lifetime. Believe, if you will, even for a moment, that there is absolutely no escape from the troubles that beset you in life at this moment in time. Do you see how this line of thinking will affect your future? Do you see how this negativity will infiltrate your mind and eat away at any chance that you may have at realizing a completely different type of life that most people are aiming for. A life filled with joy and happiness. A life filled with an unbelievable sense of God's Love and Joy and Happiness.

So how will it be for you? Will you succumb to the endless excuses that exist for being unhappy in this life, or will you somehow conjure up the strength and will, to pray to Jesus and God for a more fulfilling sense of happiness and joy that will overtake you in time; that will lead you to a more complete realization that God is the progenitor of our happiness and joy, and that His great son, Jesus, came to this very place to show us how to obtain this happiness and joy through earnest prayer to God, Himself?

Do you really think that you will have to endure the type of depression that crushes a person's spirit, and ultimately their existence in this life, or will you hand yourself over to God and His son, Jesus, in order to extricate yourself from this often terrifying existence that we seem to have to go through in this life. What will it be for you- crushing depression, or complete joy? It is a decision that we all have to make in this life; no one is immune, not even this world's wealthiest people. Do I hand my life over to God, and Jesus, in an attempt to fulfill that part of my life that is a complete failure, or do I just keep on going, hoping that my depression will not get any worse; hoping that my depression will not overtake my soul; hoping that my soul will not progress further down into that abyss known as hell? The decision is yours, and it is a decision that everyone will have to make, eventually.

PREDICTIONS

"Though I speak with the tongues of men and of angels, and have not charity, I am become as sounding brass, or a tinkling cymbal." –Paul the Apostle

The power of prediction is something that shouldn't be taken lightly and there are people, throughout time, who have had this ability in life and have accurately been able to predict the future of not only a person, as a psychic would, but of the world, as perhaps a prophet would. But the intriguing thing about the power of prediction is that it is sometimes a very misguided power.

If someone was to tell you, perhaps, something negative about your life and proclaimed that it was going to happen to you in the near future, would you believe this person; especially if they were a psychic that you had employed? And what if this event that they had predicted actually came true in your life? Would this make you a believer in the power of prediction? But what if you had never heard what this person, or psychic, had to say to you, perhaps because you never actually visited them? Would the same negative event still have occurred in your life? The truth may very well shock some people who are not aware of the power of prediction, or suggestion.

How could it be that some psychics in this world can accurately predict negative events in either a person's life or in the world itself? Maybe it is because some people, or psychics, are unknowingly or inadvertently "channeling" a very negative source of information into another person's life, or even into this world itself. What if every time we heard negative information that was given to us, we decided not to believe it? What if, instead, we chose to pray to God for His all important power of protection that He offers to us, if we just chose to pray to Him instead of believing whatever negative information that was headed our way? Perhaps we might experience a very different outcome in our lives. Instead of fearing, and perhaps eventually experiencing a negative event in our lives that was offered up to us by a psychic, or anyone else for that matter, maybe we would experience something better because of our faith in God and His protection.

Not all psychics purvey negative information, and in fact many psychics may actually help people understand many things in life through positive information that is offered to people. And this may, once again, truly go back to the power of suggestion, or even to the power of predicting positive events in people's lives. But once again, prediction itself is something that may very well be best "checked at the door."

"Not my will, but God's will be done." These are some very powerful words spoken by Jesus that could very well illustrate how important it is not to project our own desire for future knowledge, but rather embrace the peace and the joy that God has for us, right here in this moment, and beyond. If we decide to embrace God's plan for us, then there may not be any need at all to "see" what the future may have in store for us; considering that God's plan will unveil itself to us in due time.

So, as Paul the apostle inferred, nearly two millennia ago: Even though I may be able to speak in the manner of men and angels (possibly beholding things on a different level?), if I don't have charity (love?) than I am just a sound that is not beautiful (or rather, disdainful). In other words, if what I say is not truly directed by love, then it is not worth saying because of the negative power that it could carry into another person's life, or into this world itself. This too, can pertain to those who have the power of prediction in this world. If the people, or psychics in this world, that have the power of prediction are not in line with God's principles and love, then their message could very well be one that is not a beautiful one to behold and of a negative origin.

For example, if someone predicted that a powerful explosion was going to occur over the Northeastern United States, perhaps even Vermont, at some point in time, this then would be a very negative prediction that could bring very negative information into this world and possibly affect those who were to believe this prediction. Whether or not this would actually occur has yet to be seen, but an event like this would inevitably represent a power other than that of God if it were indeed going to happen. In fact any prediction along these lines could very well have a negative effect on this world and should be met with faith in God and the power of prayer.

Any number of other predictions could be made as well by anyone really. Someone could say that maybe they thought an aircraft carrier was going to sink within the near future, sparking a great war. Someone else could say that maybe the skies all across this world would soon turn a fantastic pinkish-orange color, for only one day, ushering in a new age in which love and peace would reign. Still others might predict that a great disturbance deep within our earth would trigger seven great earthquakes within a short period of time or that a massive explosion that took place in our earth's atmosphere was really an extra-terrestrial warning that if mankind did not change his destructive ways, then our world would soon end. The list of predictions could go on and on. But still the fact remains that even if these things ever did happen, God would be protecting us, either with His swift help or with His open arms upon our arrival into heaven itself. Either way, God is here...right now...and forever.

ARMAGEDDON

It happened one day when I least expected it and my life would be changed forever, as a result. There was a lot of suffering on different levels and I did not know why this had to happen. I had never seen anything like it, really. But all I knew is that this was easily the worst time of my life that I had ever experienced. It was almost as though I was going through Armageddon- but on a different level than that of this world; perhaps on the level of my soul.

There were ungodly visions and monsters that seemed to come out of nowhere, with their menacing looks and evil intentions. There were terrible nightmares and angry people who were both very disconcerting to me. There were even messages from beyond that forecast my own destruction. But what was most disturbing to me was that these things had one thing in common- they were all after the one thing that is most precious to the devil himself. I didn't realize this until later, but this was really an onslaught by the devil who was taking full advantage of everything at his disposal, in an attempt to take that thing that he wanted the most…my soul.

If it hadn't been for God's great protection and the fact that He was with me through my entire "dark night of the soul", I would not have made it through. But this is exactly why I felt like I had experienced an Armageddon at the level of my soul, because I cannot imagine a greater battle than that which is fought over a person's soul, than that which had been fought over my own soul. And this is what I would remember forever, after my own personal Armageddon was over. This experience would change me forever, but in a good way. It would forever cement God's presence within my life and would eventually lead me into another direction in life that involved writing about my experiences in life that were of a spiritual nature. And because of the nature of spiritual warfare, there were many good things that I was able to write about, but also many dark and evil things as well.

What perplexed me the most about this very dark experience, though, was that I had not known of many other people in this world who had gone through such a violent spiritual battle and on such a personal level as I had. I only had Jesus himself to look at as the model of someone who had fought such wickedness in this world that it had ultimately brought him to his end, or so it would seem. For, Jesus was able to transcend this world and become a far mightier force for good in the afterlife, especially for those of us who are experiencing trouble and tribulation right here in this world. But this still didn't satisfy my complete curiosity as to why my spiritual plight in life had been such a dark and at times, crushing experience.

I decided that instead of continually reflecting upon it, I would write about my spiritual experience in very candid terms. Because what if there were people in this world right now, who were suffering through a spiritual struggle that they had little knowledge about? What if there were people experiencing a spiritual Armageddon of their own, right now? But even more compelling to me was the idea that maybe there were people who could even avoid this personal spiritual Armageddon that the devil so wishes to cast upon any soul that he can, by learning of God's and Jesus' existence and their desire to help people even before they get into spiritual trouble. By just accepting God and Jesus into their life, many people could possibly dodge the possibility, entirely, that they would ever experience what I had experienced. But what would make people believe that there really was something of a "dark night of the soul" that actually existed in this life? Would someone really have to experience some type of spiritual discomfort in this life before they really turned to God and Jesus for help? Would the darkness really have to come to some people before their door was opened to the light that God has for each of us?

These were all questions that only time itself would be able to answer, and possibly if at all. But I was determined to write about my spiritual experiences and the things that I saw, in an attempt to help anyone who was seeking knowledge about spiritual matters. But here was the thing- anyone seeking knowledge of spiritual matters would have to detach themselves, to some degree, from this world and its daily events; its antics, you might say, that seem to distract people from what is truly real and what is eventually coming our way; either heaven…or hell.

THE ANNOUNCER

"Game on!" the announcer yelled. I was excited. I was watching a very important soccer game in the world cup on my television that was taking place during this particular year, and I could tell it was going to be a good one. Sure enough, one of the teams scored an early goal and it was indeed proving to be the type of game that I had hoped it would be. Within minutes, the other team had scored a goal that equalized the score. Wow. If you were into soccer, like I was at the time, then this was the game that you wanted to see.

But as the game progressed, I slowly began to remember the other responsibilities that had been put upon my shoulders recently that would require my greatest attention. Though my first daughter was still just an idea in our minds since she hadn't been born yet, my wife and I were completely remodeling and renovating the large Victorian style home that we had purchased a few years prior. Along with this responsibility was the ever needed income that my job as a flight attendant provided and I knew that I was going to have to fly as many hours as possible in order to meet the increased financial demand that our home renovation was putting upon us. But the greatest responsibility that I had at the time was also the one that I had been ignoring the most- that of my newly expanding spiritual experience. I didn't know it at the time, but this newly acquired spiritual responsibility would soon blossom into a very dark and difficult "dark night of the soul."

All of the signs had been there for me. The 444's, the nightmares, the ever increasing messages that were coming my way, the books that seemed to fall off the shelf in front of me while I was at any given bookstore's spirituality section, just begging me to read them, and also just the general feeling that my world was not as it had once been; a life that was sometimes boring, but albeit completely understandable and that had not had anything extraordinary interjected into it from somewhere beyond this world. Yes, you could easily say that I was "not in Kansas" anymore. And if these things weren't enough of a warning to me that my life was not on its normal trajectory anymore, then perhaps nothing would be able to spell this out for me, perhaps nothing would be able to get my attention in the way that the universe was trying to demand of me. Nothing that is, except for my demons.

When I awoke one night to see my first demon right in front of my eyes, staring back at me in a most terrifying manner, to say the least, I then knew that I was in a little bit of trouble. I was in a little hot water, you could say; hellish, hot water. This then is when I realized that I had my work cut out for me, and then some. This is the point at which I realized that I simply could not return to my previous life. Any straight line back to that previously boring, but yet enjoyable life, had been short circuited by a force that was beyond my ability to readily understand, both in its ability to interject itself right into my life through various images, dreams and somewhat violent feelings and emotions, and also in its ability to disguise the source from which it had come into my life. I would also soon discover that this was not going to end anytime soon and that these hellish visitations from beyond were going to start really getting my attention. They had finally, fully gotten my attention. But what did they want?

It would take many years for me to figure out the answer to this question. But one thing was for sure; if I didn't give this crisis my all, my complete attention, my true focus, then I was going down, literally down. Down into a darkness that my mind had no previous understanding of or a link to, down into a place that I did not know had even existed, down into a place that was eternal in its ability to confuse, terrify, cage and control, down into hell itself. It was then that I realized that I was going to have to focus on the crisis that was at hand, because it was my very soul that was at stake here. This was not a friendly game of soccer that I was playing in, just like I had enjoyed playing in many times before earlier in my life. This was not a game in which the stakes were either winning or losing a fun filled sporting event. This was a situation in which my very soul was at stake. This was a spiritual crisis in which I was playing against the devil, himself, for keeps; forever.

Once I had realized this, the decision was pretty easy to increase my focus on the spiritual matter that was at hand, exponentially you might say. In other words, I began to increase the attention that was being demanded of me by my current spiritual situation by focusing intently on what type of information was coming to me from beyond. I began to put more intention behind what I was doing in my life. By this I mean that I no longer was floating through life, only focused on those things that I wanted to do, or enjoy. Instead, I was choosing, for the first time in my life, to follow the beat of another drummer. And which drummer I would eventually end up following would be of the utmost importance to me, ultimately. Would I follow the depression, the fear, the confusion, the hopelessness and hatred of the drummer who was beating his drum with all of his wicked beats and more? Or would I follow the beat of another drummer; the one who offered me hope, love, joy, comfort, safety and a host of other wonderful things? Which one would end up ultimately leading me through the rest of my life?

"Goal! Gooooaaal!!!" The announcer's scream brought me back from these thoughts, announcing yet another goal in the hard fought game of world cup soccer that was still on my television. The camera zoomed in on all of the fans that were going absolutely wild in the stands. It gave me the feeling that this was not only going on in this stadium, but around the world as well. Because according to the television announcer, over half of the world's population was also watching this very game; over 3 billion people. But at this moment I suddenly felt isolated, alone. I knew that I was supposed to be enjoying this moment, but I also knew that I was somehow disconnected from all of these people who were watching this game, this global event. I think that at this moment in time I began to realize that I was going to have focus on other things in life besides an event like this that I had been watching, taking in, and experiencing, if I was going to survive my ever increasing spiritual crisis.

I walked over to my television and actually turned it off. Sure I could have finished watching one of the most exciting sporting events in the world, but I also knew that if I didn't maintain my focus on what was quickly reaching a boiling point in my life, I might not be around much longer to even be able to make these types of decisions in life. After all, I had been through several close calls lately that had been life and death situations. At least this is what these particular situations had left me feeling about them. There had been the situation that had occurred while I was flying as a flight attendant on an airplane, and there was also the one that involved another car while I had been driving on the highway recently. These brushes with death were enough to make me realize that I was not currently just playing a game. Rather, I was in deeper than I had ever been before, and I was going to have to give this crisis my all, my every effort, my entire focus. This game wasn't for points, it was for my soul.

AGAIN

There he was again. Except this time he was standing on a street corner that was placed just a few blocks north of the coffee shop that I was driving to. The man that I had previously seen waving at me from across the street was now placed squarely in town, in a place that seemed to command the view of every driver that was slowly creeping through this particular town. I looked at him as I passed, slowly studying him, absorbing the new look that he was sporting. A gray beard had grown in, adding to the stature that this man demanded of any observer. A cigarette still hung from his mouth, unfinished. He had a distant gaze, but still had the intent in his eyes that he had previously shown when he had been waving to me from across the street, just a few days prior to this one.

He had the demeanor of a man who hadn't been fully sunk, but was fighting the inevitable descent into something unfamiliar. Perhaps it was his "stockbroker" appearance that suggested something else, that suggested that he had at one time determined his own fate in life, perhaps with an everlasting supply of income, or some other form of comfort that was now fleeting, that gave away his true reason for standing at this corner as I drove by. Maybe it was just his stance. The carefree way in which he accepted his new direction in life was derided by his slightly wrinkled gray suit; the same gray suit that he had worn just a few days before.

But what was it that truly drew my attention to this man? Was it the way in which he had familiarized himself with his presence to me a few days before by waving at me from across the street, or was it by some other force that was bringing us together at this point? Maybe it was just in the way that he was able to simultaneously ignore and yet embrace his environment that made me think that this man was at once both out of his element, but yet at one with his surroundings. How could this be, I thought to myself?

All of these thoughts and more ran through my mind, all at once, almost as if my mind had been temporarily refocused by a higher power as I drove by this man who was standing on the corner. Why was I so fixated on him? And what was in store for us? Only God, Himself, would know, I told myself as I gently accelerated my car through the remaining three blocks to the coffee shop that I was headed towards.

TIME AND AGAIN

"O.K., that sounds good. But what does he mean by repay me?"

"He wants you to know that you are a good friend of his and always have been. He knows that you are not able to meet your needs as well as you would like to be meeting them right now, but he will make this up to you in time. He speaks of a time when you pass from this world."

"Why is he going to do this for me?"

"Because he appreciates what you are doing for him now and although he may not be able to repay you for your kindness now, he will make all this worth your while when he sees you again."

"But how did he know me? How were we good

friends?"

"At one point you told him that you wished you could change places with him when he was in a time of suffering and he appreciates your compassion towards him during this time. You were good friends with him."

"Wait…"

"Just remember that he loves you now and always…forever. He will make this up to you. He promises you this…"

As I woke up I glanced over at the digital clock that was positioned below my bed on a small filing cabinet that held important papers of mine. It read 11:11. How strange this was. It felt like I had been sleeping for hours already, but I had only recently gone to sleep at around 9:30 in the evening. This was very strange. I had seen this number many times in the past, but mostly when I was already awake. But I seemed to be waking up now more at times that would rock me from my sleep. Sometimes it was a gentle thing when I would glance at the clock and see 4:44 during the early hours of the morning. And sometimes it would seem as if I had been jarred awake. This time, though, was a gentle awakening that left me in a state of slumber. But then I remembered the dream I was having right before I had woken up.

In this dream I was talking to someone who was able to tell me what Jesus, himself, apparently wanted me to know. This was impossible, I thought to myself. How could I be speaking with someone who knew Jesus and was conveying a message to me from Jesus himself? This was very astonishing, especially since I had never really entertained the idea that I had even known Jesus or perhaps could even communicate with him, even if it was indirectly. I could only pass this off as one of those impossible dreams that left me with more questions than answers.

But I could relate to what he was saying to me in this dream. It was very easy for me to totally understand what he had been talking about. It really seemed as though he understood not only my financial struggles that I had been going through for some time, but especially the struggle that I had gone through during my "dark night." It seemed as if he really knew of the pain and complete depression that I had experienced during this time and that he was really going to make this up to me. It's not as though he even owed me anything, rather it seemed as if he truly wanted to give me something special when I saw him again. I thought to myself how this could probably only mean that I would see him again after I transitioned from this world to the next in what would be my eventual death. Funny, I thought to myself, most of the time I felt like I could wait until my death would eventually take me. But now I was more curious than ever about what lay ahead for me when my life finally would expire one day.

My thoughts sped ahead to the part of the conversation that I was having with the person that was in my dream, whom I couldn't see, but could readily understand, about how I had been a friend of Jesus before. I took this to mean that I had known Jesus in a previous life, the life that he had led when he came to this world to spread his message of peace and love. And suddenly it all made sense to me; everything that I had been going through in this life that had been so depressing to me, the frustration that I had been experiencing with finding suitable employment and all of the inane roadblocks that I had run into in my search for a job, the "dark night" that I had endured, all of the spiritual insights and lessons that I had learned from it, perhaps he had been there with me the whole time, waiting for me to accept the fact that there was something greater in this life that was planned for me. And as to what this might be, I really didn't know, other than the fact that I was now writing about all of the crazy and sometimes dark spiritual things that had happened to me in my life. It all made sense to me now…until the next morning.

I awoke that morning with a sense of vigor and happiness that lasted only a few moments until I began to really think about the possibility that I had somehow been a friend of Jesus during the time that he had walked in this world. Silliness; that is how most people would think about such a proposition, for sure, I thought to myself. And it was how I was starting to think about it myself in this moment. But a strange thing began to occur from time to time during the next couple of months. I really began to latch on to that dream for inspiration and for companionship from beyond. So many dark things had already happened to me in the past that were truly impossible. Why not this then? Why couldn't I have possibly known Jesus in the past and been a friend of his? Crazy, I thought to myself. And as to why I just couldn't get over this piece of information was really quite confusing to me, mostly because I had been so readily accepting of all of the other crazy spiritual things that had happened to me in the past. So why not this; especially since it would easily represent the most positive piece of information I had ever welcomed into my life?

I don't know why, but I decided that at least I could accept the fact that Jesus was truly helping me in this lifetime in the way that he could. And this was information that I truly needed at this point in my life, especially since I was beginning to embark on a series of writing adventures that would include some of the craziest information that some people would ever read about, concerning spiritual events from beyond this world that had affected me in the past, and it seemed, in the present as well. I was definitely going to need his help if I was not going to be laughed right out of this world, and perhaps the universe itself, after revealing what I had been experiencing throughout the past twenty years of my life that was already forty-eight years old. But now was the time. And this would be the place to make my stand. I would do this for him. And I could finally relax my mind about all of the crazy spiritual high jinks and darkness that I had gone through and continued to go through, just knowing that he was going to be waiting for me in the end; that time when I would need him the most; that time when anyone would need him the most.

But in the end, I just kept telling myself that it was only a dream, right?

THE OTHER SIDE

Sure, I had had other dreams. Like the one where a nuclear missile from the U.S. had been headed for Moscow and the fiery question that had followed, "Where are you going to go?" And they were even as vivid as the one in which I had been conversing with a person who was sent to me on behalf of Jesus, himself. But some of these other dreams were far more disturbing, to say the least. Like the one in which I had actually seen an alien figure that had been pointing a gun at me. He was actually threatening me with a gun that was of an archaic origin and it looked as if it was from the times of the Spanish conquistadors. Wow, this one was really weird. Except, in this particular dream I was looking into the eyes of the alien that was going to try and kill me with this gun that was as old as time itself. This was very strange considering alien technology was supposed to be millions of years ahead of our time; so, why the ancient gun? Maybe the correct question was why was I feeling terrified for my life? But the next thing that happened in this dream really took me by surprise, though. I yelled at the alien, "Go ahead and shoot me, kill me if you want to!"

O.K., now I was fine with death, I thought to myself, after having time to reflect on this dream. And this was not far from the truth, considering I had actually been considering taking my own life at one point during the zenith of my "dark night". But I also realized another thing at this point; I was also O.K. with the fact that at one point I had actually been afraid of the fact that maybe aliens were interfering with our lives on this planet. In other words, I had subconsciously been harboring fears within me that had to do, directly, with a fear of extra-terrestrial beings possibly interfering with my life, as well as other people's lives in this world. I began to realize though that I was willing to confront the possibility that there were actually aliens that were out there that had intentions that were not that good, perhaps even evil. And I was ready to confront not only my fears about this, but any alien that came my way, as well. How absolutely ridiculous, I thought. But apparently, this was the truth. Because how many times have dreams lied to us? For example, whenever we have fears in life, many times these are played out in our dreams that we have when we fall into that world beyond that doesn't lie to us. Whatever we experience in our dreams is most likely to be the truth, at least as far as how we actually feel about something or perceive it to be.

So, according to this dream, I was ready, not only for death, but for alien intervention itself. But how had I arrived at this point in my life? I had definitely been afraid of not only death itself, but also the possibility of any type of alien intervention in my life. Why then the sea change in my attitude concerning both of these fears that had at one point been a regular canvas upon which to exert my worst expectations in life? Death, and control; control by a higher, more powerful force; two things that I did not want in my life considering I had now been recently blessed with the birth of my first daughter.

But I had read in several books recently that a resounding and uncontestable faith in Jesus, himself, had actually saved many people from the torturous and ungodly realty of alien abduction itself. And this was not to mention the effect that a faith like this could have against the inevitable grip of death, itself. I had actually read that anyone with a powerful faith in Jesus would be spared both of these realities that this very world offered certain people. How could this be though? And I wasn't thinking about the possibility of alien abduction, no matter how outlandish this very thing might seem to certain people. I was thinking, rather, about how Jesus' protection could do just that; protect people from something as frightening as the possibility as an alien abduction.

I didn't realize it at the time, but after much further investigation into this matter through the reading of many more books, as well as divine intuition, I began to realize just how powerful Jesus was as a central spiritual figure in people's lives and in this world. He was now a complete force in this world for people who believed in him. He was completely capable of protecting people from anything that this universe had to offer, considering he was now with his Father; God, Himself.

Some people might wonder how this could be, but I began to personally realize that God was the only real power in this universe, and Jesus was the instrument, the lamb, the most powerful figure through which His power would be delivered to us. So what could this possibly mean to someone like me, who apparently was not only afraid of death, but the possibility of aliens interfering with his life in a negative way? The short answer is that I began to realize that even aliens themselves are subject to the spiritual laws of this universe that God, Himself, has laid out in front of us. In other words, there is no civilization throughout this expansive universe that can rob death of its eventual claim upon any living being. It doesn't matter how technologically advanced a certain extra-terrestrial being may be in this universe, they are all going to have to answer to death itself, no matter how many years they may live for before they die. Death, in this case, is ironically enough, the great equalizer. No amount of alien technology can save a life form from this stark and eventual reality. This is why Jesus and his teachings are apparently so profound and powerful, when taken into this context. No one shall pass unto the Father unless it is by him; by Jesus. And as far as I could tell, this included anyone here on earth as well, no matter how well off they were, no matter how much earthly power they had at their command. Once again, death would be the greatest equalizer, and no one would be immune to its effects.

So I decided to ponder this for a while. I thought about it for a week or two; then a month or so; and then finally more time passed, during which time I began to earnestly think about some of Jesus' teachings and how they could be applied to my greatest fears. Checkmate, I thought to myself. He's got them, no matter how you look at it. They all have to pass by his gate in order to get to where they want to go, eventually; heaven. I could almost imagine him sitting on a pedestal, calmly, serenely, poignantly pondering the actions of each soul, alien or not, that each had committed while alive in this universe, one at a time. One at a time, I thought? Absolutely, considering that time itself is a thing which was created and is completely controlled by God, Himself. Even an eternity would be but the blink of an eye for those who have passed into God's kingdom to serve Him as needed, or suffer as so, in a different, far removed place, if needed, if deserved, if desired by karma itself.

So here it was, all laid out for me, in the back of my head, in that part of my subconscious mind that had wrestled with concepts like eternity and infinity and even the presence of God in my life and others; the fact that someone like Jesus had come into this world to protect those people, those friends of his, that asked him for his protection. And this protection was from anything, anywhere, and at anytime. There were no exceptions. So when the alien in my dream had pointed his weapon at me in an attempt to scare me, kill me, I just yelled back at him, "Go ahead," not fearing the consequences, not fearing the end result. And according to the world in which I had been having this dream, the world in which truth is king and the truth of our subconscious thoughts rule the way in which our dreamy reality plays itself out, this was no lie; I was simply no longer afraid of death or of alien intervention. It's true…the power of Jesus had entered into my soul…and in a big way.

MICHAEL

There it was again, that word. How bizarre, I thought to myself. I had been used to synchronicity occurring in my life almost on a regular basis at this point. Even though I did not know exactly what kind of message was going to be behind any given type of synchronicity that occurred in my life, you could definitely say that I was the victim of some type of ultra, out of this world, synchronicity that was playing itself out in my life. I was like a deer that was caught in the headlights at this point, you might say. Even those who could not understand my plight in life, my spiritual conundrum, my darkest of nights, had to admit that the things that I was seeing were literally out of this world; that is if they chose to believe me. That is why I stopped explaining myself to people and instead just chose to ride out the currents of ridiculous spiritual information that were coming my way; one long ride, one long trip, one long dream.

There were times when I was inundated with the same word through an unrelenting series of synchronistic events in my life that would lead me straight down the line, down that line that leads into a train itself, almost. The headlights of information would be blaring at me from beyond and all I had to do was connect the dots. In other words, there it was for me, right in front of me, the information that I needed to assimilate in order to understand a new message that was obviously aimed at me from beyond, from another world, you might say; but why me? I asked myself this question a hundred times at least, and every time, silence; no answer from a higher power, no answer whatsoever, only the information, the very important information.

And so it was with the word "Michael". So what, I thought to myself. This message obviously has to do with my little buddy Michael, I thought. Because, at the time, I was engaged in the act of supervising a ten year old boy named Michael, with whom I was actively mentoring. Michael only had his mother in life with which to depend upon until I entered his life. I only spent a few hours at a time with him every week, and sometimes even a day. But this was time that was meant to be spent with him in an effort to provide a positive role model for him in life.

It was before my first daughter had been born and it was a lot of fun. Michael and I would frequent all of the best places that southern New Hampshire had to offer, at least as judged by a ten year old boy. We went to the water parks, the arcades, the pizza places, the ice cream places and everything in between. It was more fun than we had a right to enjoy, I thought at times. But all the while I thanked God for His blessing, not only upon this boy, but upon me as well. For I was learning; learning about the intricacies that are involved with the world of a child and all of the things that could go wrong instantaneously, especially with a child with ADHD; but also about all of the things that were as right as rain, all of the impossibly joyous events cast upon us by a higher power. This was a time in which I was learning about, and also enjoying, God's unlimited power to deliver joy into this world, my world.

It would be unfair for me to say that I was jealous of this boy that I was taking care of once a week. But I began to realize that this very boy had somehow inherited the joy of God as his birthright. Or maybe it was just the combination of the both of us together that created a nebula of fantastic possibilities when it came to beating the arcade games themselves that had been placed there to beat us, as well as anything else that we put our minds to. How could this be? How could we have been placed together to beat not only the system, but the devil himself? The devil himself...? Wow...

The next thing I realized, I was involved with not only one Michael, but two. I realized this one night when I had been having a dream about the archangel Michael, himself. In this dream, I remember I was talking to him, about what, I don't even remember to this day. But he was there, with all his power. And then all of a sudden, without reason or delay, I began to continue the dream in which I had been talking to Michael, the pinnacle of power, with a very funny but everlasting dreamt memory in which I was sliding down the longest water slide in the universe with my little buddy Michael. It was as if the archangel Michael had incarnated himself into the boy that I had been involved with as a mentor for the past year and a half, in this particular dream. This was really wild. This was completely unimaginable. But in the short period that my dream was being created by some higher power, I'm sure, I had the distinct feeling that I was a friend of Michael, the archangel; Michael, my new friend; Michael my new discovery.

This was crazy. I was now the friend of Michael, my little buddy, and Michael, the archangel. And to add to this confusion, was the fact that I had just visited Michael, the clairvoyant. He was the only psychic that I had ever physically met in my life, while searching for answers that would haunt me way beyond my visit to him. But he was good, he was really good. No negative information about my future, no terrible predictions, only the good stuff, like clogged gutters; clogged gutters. I went home after my visit to him only to discover that I truly did have some clogged gutters like he had intuited that had been causing a torrent of rain to enter into my garden, flooding any form of vegetation in its path.

But Michael had also told me some things that would last with me until this day. "It's your turn to write" he told me. My turn to write, I thought? "O.K.", I said, "but about what?"

AN ARMY OF ONE

There he was again. It was the archangel Michael. But this time he was burning brightly in my dream. He appeared to me as a little boy would, but with the power of the universe wrapped up in his being. His very bright blue eyes appeared to me as burning blue iridescent globes. They were bright, but like the eyes of an animated child. As to why he appeared to me like this, I have no idea. It was almost as if he did not want to disturb me, make me fearful, even though I was being visited by the pinnacle of angelic power, himself. The same bright blue eyes that would burn through any evil, I thought. But these were the eyes of someone who was my friend, someone who was an archangel.

But why, then, did I also have a dream in which I actually saw myself staring back at none other than myself, only several nights later, especially since I was as animated in this dream as Michael had been, in a way. But yet there I was, my grey eyes shining brightly, just as Michael's had a few nights before, a few dreams before. But what was the purpose of this? Why was I staring into the eyes of a stranger, the eyes of someone that I had known so well, the eyes of someone who, really, was my best friend; myself? And why were my green eyes now grey in this dream? I suppose I could have asked the same thing about Michael, himself. Why was he coming to me? Why was I looking into his eyes as someone who I actually knew, even though no one would believe me, even if I had gone to great lengths in which to describe him? And why did I feel so isolated when I thought about all of these things? No one believed me, no one thought I was sane when I talked about these things, which waned with time, considering the repose that most people offered me when I approached them with such information. Just why did I feel as if I had been thrown into an arena that consisted of many demonic opponents, and no allies? No allies, whatsoever.

I often times pictured myself as a lone Spartan, as someone who had been lost from the ranks of an army that had long since departed in its effort to locate and engage an unknown enemy. I felt as though I was perched high above this world, in a realm in which not many people had any knowledge about. Sure, there were the church ministers that I had gone to in an attempt to gain some insight into the unholy spiritual events that I had been going through. But I could see from the way that they were looking at me and from the questions that they were asking me, that I was most likely possessed, in their opinion, and maybe what they had been thinking wasn't far from the truth. There were the psychics that I had either gone to, or phoned from a distance, in order to glean half a vision of what I had been trying to put together. But they told me that two and two were five, and that if I just believed in them everything would be alright. They said it was just something that I had to work out. It was just some evil within me that I had to exercise; it was just something that I had to pay them for in order to rightfully understand.

But as time went on, I began to feel even more isolated. I felt almost as a seed that is blown across this world would feel as it finally settled into the soil of another culture, the way of a strange and unwelcome new world. I could almost understand how it would have felt to have landed on the moon itself; alien, new; new in the way as in unnerving, alien, completely alien. And this was what I had to deal with. I was definitely on my own when it came to existing in this world, no matter what otherworldly creatures, imagined or real, had been unleashed upon me. I was on my own, and this would remain in my mind for some time to come, almost an eternity if you wanted to count the seconds, themselves, the moments that lied to me, the moments that said that I would be fine, if I just believed; just believed in the mumbo-jumbo, the spiritual crossroads that always led to nowhere, to another spiritual crises, to another mental breakdown.

And so it was this game that I had been engaged in; me against the world, a world which had been turned upside down. Yes, I was on my own. And I knew this on a different level. It was a level on which my own common sense resided on. It was a level on which I could somehow discount all of the fantastically crazy spiritual events that had been coming my way as something that was definitely not from this world. It was also a level on which I began to "level" my own lance, if you could actually say this. It was a level on which I began to realize that I was an army unto myself, an army of one. I was at once alone with this world and the world beyond, but completely in control of my worst fears, my most terrifying demons, my most debilitating hallucinations borne of another place and intensity, borne of the devil, himself. And I was loyal only to myself, only to that place in my mind that harkened back to the time in which I had been born into this world, loyal only to the original me, that person that had entered into this world as a solid entity, unfettered by the devil's confusion, unimpressed by the demons that he had unleashed upon my soul. I was truly an army of one, an army that was bent on reclaiming the peace that had been lost in my world, the love that had been stolen from my heart, the joy that had been replaced by an unrelenting sense or source of beguiled treachery. I was definitely on my own, an army of one.

A DIFFERENT TIME

There was a time in my life when everything was different for me. Actually it was more of what someone might call a more normal life. But from my perspective now, it was a very different time for me. It was laced with happiness and covered in that feeling which is very carefree. Bare feet, shorts and a t-shirt were the only things that I needed in order to enjoy that part of my life that I am actually talking about.

It was in a small town in Wisconsin in which this part of my life played itself out. Elm Grove was the type of place that you wanted to be growing up in during the seventies, especially where we had lived. Our house was right across the street from the elementary school that my brothers and I had attended, and beyond this school was an area of woods with a stream cutting through it that led into a stretch of fields. Beyond these fields lied the city greens that included a park, pond, swimming pool and a library. And beyond this was the small town of Elm Grove in which there were shops and stores that offered a ten year old boy like myself the opportunity to obtain anything from kites to candy, model airplanes to chocolate malts, as well as an opportunity to explore his surroundings that were far from home, according to how he saw things at the time.

My friends and I would leave our neighborhood in the warm mornings that the summertime offered and would play outside until the late afternoon sun would warn us of our parent's discontent with the fact that we had missed lunch and hadn't checked in with them for hours, for most of the day. But this was a time and a place that was both safe and secure from the modern day menaces that unfortunately make up our world today. And we would be gone for hours, enjoying the hours that our beautiful surroundings offered us. There were the fields with their six foot tall grass that had gone from green to gold over the course of the summer and that hid our four foot frames in what seemed to be hundreds of acres of land in which to discover ourselves and our new found freedom.

These were the best of times for me and my friends. They were times in which we had no responsibilities in life, no cares in life and they were also times in which time itself took on a different feeling, a feeling of time being bent in our favor, bent towards forever, because that's how those days seemed to feel, almost like they had lasted for an eternity. There were no deadlines to deal with, no heavy responsibilities lying upon our shoulders, no harsh realities that were waiting to be discovered by us. There were only streams to be waded in, tall grass forts to be played in and an unlimited possibility of dreams fulfilled within our expansive grounds in which we played, in which we had lived in, until the years began to move on for us.

We eventually grew up and went our own ways in life. And this brought with it a sense of disjointedness. A sense that somehow we were headed in a different direction than that of our tall grass forts, a different direction than that of the fish we caught, the kites we flew, the bikes we rode. We were each headed in a direction that was more mandated by adulthood, than anything else, really. However, some of us were headed in an entirely different direction than anything that we had ever learned about in school and that could ever have prepared us for in life.

This became evident to me when I had reached the age of about twenty six years of age. It was at about this point when I reached the beginning of what would become my "dark night." No one had ever mentioned this to me as being a possibility in someone's life. No one had ever taught me that there were things in this world that were of such an un-Godly origin that a person's whole life could become rocked; rocked beyond recognition. No one had ever said to me, "Joshua, be careful…be careful of what lurks beyond this world, what lurks beyond your imagination." No one had ever said that to me.

So it was when things unimaginable started happening to me that I pretended not to notice, not to notice the unimaginable. Instead, I chose to run; run to that part of my life that had always offered me a safe haven, run to that part of my life which had always been dependent upon my parents and all those things that had served me so well, the tall grass, the cold stream, the endless fields. I relied on a time gone by, a time that had already passed. I relied on the sense of comfort that had been derived from those things known as dependability, predictability and sensibility. I just knew that within this very world there was a place in which I could return in order to reclaim a sense of selfhood, a sense of comfort, a sense of peace. But what I didn't realize was that there was a force, a dark force, that was coming my way, that would negate everything I knew, everything I had believed in, everything I had played with, and within. This force would challenge me in a way that would crush my memories and that would destroy everything I had been able to depend upon. And it was bent upon not only the destruction of my memories, but of my very existence as well; my existence that had been forged by a sense of freedom, a sense of playfulness, a sense of innocence, a sense of joy.

In the end it would have its way with me. It would run wild with my spirit and my soul. It would change forever who I was. But just what was this thing? Could it truly be chalked up to that of a thing that was not of this world? Could it truly be chalked up to that of a thing that was evil? At first look it would definitely be given a judgment of that which was only evil. It would definitely be given a judgment of that which was powerful. And it would definitely have been given a medal of honor in that category in which most people would describe it as having been destructive to the soul, destructive to that part of a person which had been previously connected to freedom, joy and happiness. But just why was this happening to me? Why was I being challenged by a higher force? Weren't there other people in this world upon which to pick? Weren't there other people upon which to impose a new sense of evil, a new sense of change, a new sense of hopelessness?

I didn't know it at the time, but there was a reason for all this. There was a reason for all of this destruction on the level of my soul. For I was being transformed into that which was of another entity, another being, another persona. I was being toyed with by a higher power. I was being thrashed around by a force that had no interest in my well being, only the end results that would accommodate its perfect outcome, an outcome only marred by my inability to accept what had been laid upon my feet; power itself.

So what was I to do with my new found sense, after I had overcome my "dark night?" What was I to do with my new persona? What was I to do with what the universe was demanding of me? Change...change yourself...change the world...change your soul. And so it remained. What should I do? Change my soul? Change the world? Change my perspective? But how could I? I had enjoyed that which any child would demand of their parents, demand of their Protector. I had enjoyed that which had transformed my soul from that which was meek, into that which was powerful. I had enjoyed freedom, happiness, joy, innocence, and life; life itself. But now I was going to pay the price, the price of all this previous luxury, the price of all this happiness. Or was I?

It's true I had been confronted by a higher power. But what was its endgame? What was its purpose? And why had I been changed so irrefutably from that of an innocent boy into that which was a conqueror, a conqueror on a different level, a conqueror of all things evil, a conqueror of that which was opposed to

God? And why did these terms now satisfy me? Why did the term conqueror seem to apply to me in such an orderly way? Why did this seem to encompass my vision, my mission from God? Why was it that I had been chosen to obliterate that which was in my way, as far as the wars were concerned, as far as unhappiness was concerned, as far as corruption was concerned? Just why was this?

I had decided to play along. I had decided to write what was necessary in order to connect the dots; the dots of a higher power. I had decided to succumb to that which was necessary in order to change not only myself, but others as well. I had decided to completely change the direction in which I was headed in order to become the new poster boy of change, the new direction in which people would be headed, a direction in which anyone would perhaps find a path that was more oriented towards God, Himself.

So I embraced that which was called for in me in order to become a new person, a new soul. I embraced those thoughts that had previously led me in a direction that was self-destructive, that was wholly destructive, that was destructive of not only my soul, but my surroundings. And this included the people that I loved, the people that I served; the people that I served? Yes, even those people that I had served as a flight attendant, as a father, and as a servant of God; a servant of God? Yes, even as a servant of God...

Because as time wore on, I realized that I could not hide within the confines of a tall grass fort, I could not hide within the confines of my mother's love, I could not hide within the confines of a perfect childhood setting in which to play, in which to grow. I simply could not dodge that which was headed my way, that which was part of the design, the design of a higher power. For, my life had become a project, a project that was designed to take this world by surprise, a project that was aimed at eradicating the poverty, the destruction, the un-holiness that had invaded this very world. My life had been sacrificed on another level, by another power, in order to save that which was precious to God, that which was sacred to His creation; life itself, joy itself and love itself.

And as I slowly awoke, I realized that this vision that I had been having of my early childhood, had been suddenly imbedded indelibly into my consciousness. But why did it seem so real? Why did it seem so relevant? Why did it seem so needed...so needed by over six billion people?

MY DEATH

Die. Pretty crazy… and especially since I had just seen this word on the license plate of a car that had pulled right in front of me while I was navigating my way down a back road in New Hampshire. Why had someone put this word on their license plate? Or maybe I had just subconsciously concocted this word in an attempt to focus on something that had been running through my mind, lately. It had been a pretty messed up time for me lately with all of the demons and the messages from beyond, and the thought of death itself seemed to be a pretty good option from my current spiritual vantage point.

But I looked ahead at the car that I was now following and was certainly staring at this word on its license plate; "die." Within minutes of this car having pulled in front of me, I began to realize that I was lost. Maybe it was because of the attention that I had been paying to the license plate in front of me, or maybe it was just because the keen sense of direction that I had always possessed in life had been withered by this latest revelation; die. But I was lost. So I pulled my car off of the road on which I was currently driving and turned down a very narrow road in an effort to turn my car around and drive towards where I had just come from. But as I slowly advanced down the dusty, rocky, narrow road, I could not find any place to turn my car around. As I slowly moved towards the end of this road, I could faintly make out a clearing that was ahead, through the woods that was on all sides.

As I pulled up to the end of this road I realized that I had just embarked upon a graveyard that seemed to be hundreds of years old. The gravestones had been grayed by the centuries and the etched letters that told of a different time had been worn. I focused on the small cemetery. Maybe there were twenty headstones, maybe there were thirty. But my mind began to wander. I thought about the license plate that I had just seen and how it all seemed to seamlessly transform the scenery that I had previously been enjoying, into a graveyard that had somehow interjected itself right into my consciousness. I looked at the dates etched upon the headstones. 1853. 1875. 1998. Yes 1998- I pictured the current year as well as my name upon one of the headstones. It was going to happen, I thought to myself; but when and how?

Little did I know that I was hurtling right towards a certain death that would soon find me and strangle me with its weight, with its unrelenting will, with its untold resources and with its inevitable arrival into my life. But I didn't realize this until later, sometime after this somewhat eerie event that I had just envisioned upon a backdrop that was centuries old. It was perhaps forgotten by most, but resurrected on this day by a haunting force that had provided me with all that I needed to see in order to realize that I was now headed down a different road in life that would soon be serving me with a different reality, a reality that involved a certain death.

So there I was, dead in my tracks, at least dead in my mind. The vision was horrible. But I was not afraid to die, at least not in the typical sense, at least not in the way that most people fear dying. And this is what was very perplexing to me. Here I was facing my eventual death, my gravestone from the future, and I could have cared less. "So what," I thought to myself, "let it happen." But those words were golden to a higher power, a higher force. Those words were the incense upon which the death that I would experience would rise up to heaven itself. It was the smoky reality of disillusionment from which I would soon discover another form of death; that form which takes from a person, forever, a part of them that has been deemed necessary by the force that is operable on all levels in their mind, by that force that has many names. But death came to my mind when I transcended above my fear and gave myself to this force, this force that proclaimed itself to be a warrior from heaven, a warrior of God.

So I let go. I let go of all those things which had me tethered to this world. My fears, my angst, my lust, my lack of faith, my depression, my unfocused state, my inability to earn, my anger, my confusion, my uncompromised sense of earthly reality, my sorrow, my hopelessness…yes, my lust; my lust for all things in this world, all things material, all things limited. Limited in the sense that they were a slave to this world and its timeline, limited in the sense that they all had a point at which they would be useless to a person who was dying, but dying in a spiritual way. All of these things and more were of no use to me when I believed that there was a higher power that was operating in my life on a level on which I was not accustomed to. This was a level that I had not experienced before because of my inability to accept the death of all of these things and more from my soul, my spirit, my mind.

This death of a new order left me in a state of belittlement. It left me in a state of such incomprehensible powerlessness, that I felt as though my life in this world was wasted. I felt as though my life in this world had been wasted, without cause, without regard, without any sense, without any plan, without any reason. I felt as though my life had been reduced to a pile of mud, or at least that the power within me had faded to such a level; a pile of mud.

But what I didn't realize at the time was that I was emptying myself of all those things that would block God's true power from entering into my life, my soul, my spirit, my mind. Yes, I had become that which was worse than the dirt that lies upon our earth. I had become mud. The mud which sticks upon those who abhor this world, the mud which is spoken about under the breath of those who have labored hard to make it into the type of society that no longer believes in dirtiness and that no longer believes in things lower than that of the earth itself. Mud…

But that was me. That was how I had become. When someone was angry with me, I just cowered. When someone swore at me, I just retreated into that part of me that was powerless. Powerless to respond, powerless to understand such torment without recourse and powerless to understand just why or how I had been left in this state. It's true that, previously, I had at one time been under the influence of this world and its expectations. When someone had swung at me, I had swung back. When someone had gotten mad at me, I had gotten mad at them. When something wasn't right, I had tried to fix it.

When something had invaded my space, I pushed back.

But now everything was upside down. When I was threatened, I just backed off. When I had nothing, I did nothing. When people were angry, I just relaxed; relaxed with a sense of such an inability to do anything about it, that I just wished I were somehow like I had once been. For, I had once been that person who had a grip on his reality. I had once been that person who had it all together. There was no need to get upset, get mad, get even, because everything was alright in my life, everything was at equilibrium.

So I lived in my new state for a while. I discovered that my power had left me, my power had vanished, my cup had been emptied; my cup had been emptied…I was no more than that which was disgusting, at times, to humanity itself. People would go out go out of their way to show me how angry they were at me, how unimpressed they were with what I had become in this life. It was almost comical in the way that they had turned on me. And just who were these people, these strangers, the actors in my comedy of errors in which I was the central character?

All I knew was that things just had to change. They had to become more balanced. God just had to listen to me. I just had to pray. And so it was. I prayed for happiness, I prayed for justice, I prayed for joy, I prayed for protection, I prayed for love, I prayed for all those things that I thought would change my world. And I prayed some more, for this was what I was left with in life…prayer itself.

But what I hadn't realized at the time was that I had just killed a part of myself that was tied to this world. In fact I had just killed several parts of my being that had been anchored to this reality that demanded a certain belief, a belief that everything that happened in this world was derived from a certain point of view, a point of view that demanded retribution, that demanded a reaction, that demanded a certain lifestyle, that demanded an attention to that which was not tied to God or to heaven itself. So I changed; I changed what I did, and I prayed some more.

It was when I began to realize that my prayers were going to be answered by a force that was more powerful than anything I had previously understood in my life before, that I became tongue tied, speechless, you could say. The things that started to happen to me in my life were all things borne of a power that I had yet to fully tap. In other words, I had only begun to understand my sense of need, or want, in this world, under the terms that had somehow mystically materialized within my mind. I began to realize some of the most powerful answers to my prayers that I had ever experienced. I began to realize that I had tapped into something more powerful than life itself. But how could this be? Why were my prayers more important at this point in my life than they had been in the past? In other words, why were my prayers now being answered in such a powerful way, a way that eclipsed all other attempts at conveying my wishes, my wants, my needs, to God, Himself? Just why was He listening to me now?

…I had become mud, my glass had been emptied. And now it was being filled; filled with wishes, filled with wants, filled with happiness, filled with protection, filled with love, filled with anything good that I wanted, anything good that was within God's scope of universal will. Not my will, but God's.

So just what was God's will? I would poke, I would prod, I would pray, even for the silly things in life. But they all started to come true, at least all of those things that really meant something to me, those things that I had fought for, those things that I had turned my cheek to, those things that were inherent to all people in this world. Things like peace and prosperity, pollution and governmental power, poverty and sickness, war and destruction, greed and control. I prayed for all of these things to either flourish, or come to an end. I prayed for only good things to enter into the people's lives that were currently experiencing this world's dilemmas, this world's worst times ever.

But these prayers hadn't been answered. These

prayers hadn't been realized. These prayers hadn't been…

I stopped this line of thought and began to remember the time that I had waged a war upon myself. The time that I had become a conqueror, a conqueror that had only waged war upon the worldly things that were tied to my soul; things like hatred, envy, sorrow, hopelessness, fear, desire, lust, greed, confusion, and power…power of an earthly origin. I had killed them all and now my sights were set on a higher mission, a more important outcome, an outcome upon which many lives were dependent upon, an outcome that would only be answered by prayer and dedication; dedication to that which God, Himself, wanted me to do; to that which only God, Himself could do.

STUCK

There I was, substituting in a high school classroom. This time it was Spanish. "Que pasa" I said quietly to myself. Sure, I had been to Venezuela over twenty years ago, working with an organization whose ambitions, as far as I could tell, were to help the poorest of the poor in Venezuela. My job there was going to be to help the indigenous people of a very small Venezuelan village to dig new latrines. Along with carefully placing cocoa beans on the dusty roads that ran through their village, this was the one job that I was responsible for, and we were going to be doing this particular job with only shovels. But this wasn't a bad job. I had access to the sun which beat down upon me just north of the equator and I also had access to some of the best food that I had ever eaten. Whatever the spices were that were used in the meals that the locals had given us to eat was off the charts as far as the taste that they provided. Along with the excellent food, plentiful sunshine and international companionship was a sense of pride that I had accomplished something in life that not many people had done. I was here to help some of the poorest people in this world and this is what I was all about in my early twenties.

This need to help people would continue on through my life, though, all the way into my present life. And here I was, standing in front of a classroom of high school students as a substitute teacher for the local high school Spanish teacher. This is where my life had led me, over twenty years after my experience in Venezuela. Very ironic, I thought to myself. Had I come full circle? Had I finally reached the bottom of my career by substitute teaching? In terms of money actually earned, I was still better off at this point, because my experience in Venezuela had been for free. I had been a volunteer. But now I was making a bit above minimum wage as a substitute teacher. But more irony cascaded through my mind. I couldn't help it. It just flowed through my consciousness. And finally I let myself succumb to the twisted irony that bellowed out to anyone who had been paying attention to my life for the past several years. I was one of the most qualified substitute teachers that had ever stepped in front of this class, at least if you were following the level of education that I had attained, if not for the fact that I couldn't speak fluent Spanish. It's true that at this point in my life I had obtained my master's degree in education and was on the lookout for a full time job.

But as things progressed, I seemed to get caught up in the mired mess that too much substitute teaching can offer someone with higher aspirations in life. It happened one day when I was caught off guard, actually investigating my latest pay stub, only to see that I hadn't even broken the minimum wage mark when it came to working a five day week. The sad fact remained that I had been substitute teaching for over five years at this point in my life. But even sadder, to me, was the fact that I had been totally ignoring one piece of important information in my life; that my future was tied into something greater than that of just an ordinary paycheck. I had been ignoring the fact that I had weathered a "dark night of the soul" that would make any dark spiritual tale that someone could possibly relate to me, as being only second tier, as far as its intensity and dark information that could possibly be revealed. I had also been ignoring the fact that maybe there was an entirely different type of employment that I should be seeking in this world, other than that of an overly qualified substitute teacher.

But why was this? I knew that I had an insatiable desire to fit in with any crowd that I decided to run with in life. But I also knew that if I were to affiliate myself with the type of crowd that was willing to abandon all logic and normality in their search for a different type of existence, an existence that demanded a spiritual affiliation with a higher power, then I was going to have to abandon my attempt at any type of normal life, and this apparently would include a normal paycheck. At least this is what a higher power would have me believe and it seemed as though this higher power, itself, was all too happy to help redirect me in my life with a cacophony of catastrophic financial events that seemed to derail any attempt I had made in life at leading a normal life. Yes, it would seem as if the type of paycheck I was seeking would have to wait, perhaps infinitely so in terms of time; time spent on chasing a job that would support my family's needs in life, and maybe even some of their wants. But once again, the question haunted me, "Why?"

The only sense that I could make of all this was to write; write about my experiences in life that all led down the same path, that all led through hell, that all led to God. No money…no problem. Just sit down and write. Just think and obey. Just type and observe…observe the spiritual truths that graced the paper upon which I wrote.

And God's universal sense of irony had not been lost on me when, one day, as a long term substitute teacher for another teacher who had left for a different job, I sat staring ahead at the wall that was in front of the desk that I was seated at. I had just found out that the teaching position that I had been substitute teaching for, long term, was going to be eliminated for the next school year. And I had been giving this long term substitute job all of my effort for almost three months, but apparently it was for naught; for the teaching position, itself, was no longer. As I sat staring ahead, I slowly, ever so slowly, started to focus on the words that lied across the room I was in, on a portable white board. As I slowly let my lazy gaze turn into something sharper, I focused upon the letters W-R-I-T-E. These were the only letters on the white board that was across the room, apparently left there by another teacher, at another time.

It made sense though. These were the letters that formed a word that was the only thing in life that now seemed to make sense to me- WRITE. And so it became. I started to write about even more things that I had gone through during my "dark night" that seemed to have engulfed over half of my life in some way, shape or form. Even if it wasn't the actual spiritual madness that had encompassed a large part of my life, it was also the redirection by a higher power during the continuation of my life after my "dark night" that somehow seemed to offer a seamless, tumultuous and very lengthy period of time that had overrun my life with impossible frustration, at times, with how my financial situation had gone from good to bad, to worse. But this was the way in which God was going to direct me in life. And I knew that there was probably no great lottery of earnings awaiting me at the end of my journey, even if I yielded to God and wrote, and wrote, and wrote. I only knew that writing was the only thing that made sense to me now. And anything that made sense to me was a gift at this point; a veritable treasure of common sense that seemed to stick its own nose up to all of those things that had violated me, confounded me, vexed me to no end.

So I wrote. I wrote every night. I even took a day or two off from substitute teaching, in order to write, though we needed money badly. And I wrote about everything. I wrote about spiritual things as well as mundane, everyday things. I wrote when I wasn't feeling well. I wrote when it was late at night. I even wrote when I should have been doing other things, like getting ready for work. Crazy, absolutely crazy, I thought to myself. But this was urgent, it was on the front burner, and someone, other than me, wanted this to be known, to be written. I will oblige, no doubt, I thought to myself, because this is the only thing that makes sense to me now.

Had I lost my mind? Had I really been reduced to that of a shell of a person, the shell of a soul, that was hunkered down in front of a PC, tapping away at its keys, knowing all along that this would bring no money, no source of income? And the fact that my family was hurtling along into that part of the year, the summer itself, in which we had zero chance of making ends meet only added to this sense of urgency. Maybe I could get this all down on paper before my substitute teaching opportunity dried up at the end of the current school year, and then I could get a summertime job. No way, I thought. There was just too much coming my way, too many thoughts, too many demands on a spiritual level, too many unanswered questions that had to be sifted through in order for my task to be finished, perhaps even too many potential people who would need access to the type of information that was flowing through me at the speed of thought.

So I typed as fast as I could and with all the intent that a person could conjure. I typed as often as I could, so that this command of God's would be gone, perhaps, gone when this book was gone that I was now typing; gone to a publisher, gone to somewhere else, other than my laptop. Only then would this inane sense of sensibility be gone for good, I thought. Only then would I be able to regain my thoughts, my mind, my own will to rise every morning and do something else, do something other than write, do something other than that which God, Himself, had planned for me to do; do something other than make less than minimum wage in my hunt to satisfy my family's needs, in order to satisfy my most innate of needs, in order to satisfy God, Himself.

ONCE UPON A TIME

So there I was again, in front of another classroom of students. One of the students came up to me and said, "Excuse me, Mr. W, but I need to go to the bathroom."

"O.K., honey, just remember to close the door behind you."

She was as cute as a petunia. At least this is how I had referred to my daughters when they had been this particular girl's age; cute as a petunia. As this girl quickly walked towards the bathroom that was located within the classroom that I was substitute teaching in, I surveyed the situation that was rapidly unfolding in front of me. Book bags were flying in every direction. Folders being wildly taken out of cubby holes and thrown towards the tables that would soon accommodate my students. In fact chaos itself had assumed a role in this classroom that must have been pretty much standard, I thought to myself.

I noticed all of the signage that had been placed upon the walls of this particular classroom. One sign read, "Fairytales are what dreams are made of", and yet other signs read, "Mother Goose" and "Humpty Dumpty." It seemed as if there was a theme that had been started in this room by the teacher that had regularly occupied this classroom. Fairytales, I thought. Fairytales… but on this very day it would make sense to me like at no other time and in ways that I could only begin to explain to myself as the day wore on.

So I continued with the day's agenda.

"Since we are all in kindergarten for a full day at this point, who would like to explain the day's agenda to the rest of our class."

"I would Mr. W."

"Then come on up and show everyone what we will be doing today."

The boy of five years of age walked up to the front of the class and proceeded to explain to everyone what the day would look like as far as what we would be doing as a class. He proceeded to announce the first subject which would be math. Then he explained that spelling would follow this subject, followed by reading and then recess. After explaining to the class just what the schedule would be for the day, he sat down.

"Thank you Tyler. Let's begin math. Can anybody tell me what two plus two is…?"

The day wore on. I was tired. I had been fighting a cold that was in its second week and had not let go of the grip that it currently had on my reserves of energy. Even in front of the class while I was standing up, talking, I could feel my will to teach begin to wane, more and more as the day wore on. And this feeling only became worse.

By the time recess and lunch had rolled around, I was completely drained of energy. O.K., I can keep going, I thought to myself. And sure enough, I was able to make it until my class went to their daily "specials" class. Today it would be music. Yes, I silently said to myself. Now I can have fifty minutes of free time to myself. Fifty minutes to do whatever I want to do. But what happened next was beyond explanation, as far as its clarity and sense of possibility. The truth of what happened next was magnified way beyond reason, the gravity of the vision was overwhelming.

It happened after I had dropped my students off at their music class and I had returned to my desk where

I thought I would read for a while. But as I began to read, I also began to fall asleep, with the weight of my sickness finally putting me down. Not a good thing if you are a substitute teacher. Not a good thing if you are trying to become a teacher.

As I nodded my head upwards and wearily looked at the sign across the room that read "Fairytales are what dreams are made of", my vision began to waver. My mind began to translate what my eyes were seeing into a strange mix of reality and confusion, dreaminess and weight, the kind of weight that seems to drag you down into the world of another way, a way that speaks about silliness and laughter, dancing and dreaming; if only this could last for a million years…

I jerked my head upright, surveying the classroom for my students. O.K., they were all in music class. No problem, they are taken care of for a while, I thought. And then it happened as my head went down, again.

A vision of monstrous proportions flashed through my mind. There was a dragon that was shooting a bright orange and yellow fire at a king that was seated on his thrown. It immediately reminded me of the demonic visions that I had had years ago. It made me sit straight up in my seat. I awoke again, but this time I was still in that state of mind that lies somewhere in between sleep and reality. And I began to imagine many things that were somehow very real. I immediately imagined the leaders of this very world confronting their very own dragons, their very own demons. I saw how real this possibility could be and in my current slumberous stupor I had begun to become confused…wait, was this happening now, or was this going to happen in the near future? But more came to me in my state of mind. I began to realize how unfair it had been, perhaps, that I had undertaken such a deep and dark period of my life, while other people like our world's current leaders had seemed to coast through life, starting wars, crushing economies, and killing innocent men, women and children with their current treacherous policies; policies that were always borne of greed and fear or just plain power hungry plans put into place in order to rule the world.

But why would this very thing happen to the leaders of this world? Why would they, themselves, have to go through a "dark night of the soul." And why was it going to be so tough, so dark, so dangerous to their very souls according to my vision. After all, I hadn't called for this vision. I hadn't wished this upon them. I didn't even know them and nor did I wish any evil upon them.

And while I did wish for a better world from time to time, I had generally acknowledged to myself that nothing could help this world or its leadership.

Nothing could aid the boisterous decisions that now seemed so commonplace within this world, that now seemed to destroy more and more hope of ever becoming a world unto which God, Himself, would be pleased to call His own.

It's true, I had also acknowledged that a person's spiritual task in this life was to try and become as close to God as possible, in order to escape this prison of despair, this global prison of death, destruction and desertion; desertion of all ideals that had anything to do with God's principles in life. For there was no joy, there was no happiness, there was no love, there was no food, there was no shelter, there was no peace, there was no innocence, there was no shine of God's light upon the majority of this world anymore.

And while anyone could argue that all of the darkness in this world was all necessary for any soul to transcend beyond this madness into heaven, that this was all necessary for any soul to learn from when it came to spirituality, that it was necessary to experience the darkness before the light, it still seemed that this particular vision that I was having had more to do with the future of God's creation, then with anything else. This vision tempted me with the possibility that there were actually other people in this world that were going to go through what I had gone through, a "dark night of the soul." And to be honest about it all, I couldn't imagine what type of terrifying visions were being reserved for those who had defiled God's children themselves. After all, throughout my lifetime, I had done some things that I was not proud of, and that I had to come clean about, spiritually speaking. But I had never pulled the trigger on hundreds of thousands, or even millions of innocent lives, in this world. And I was thinking only of our current global situation, not to mention all of the atrocities that had happened throughout this world's past.

So who would break this pattern of violence that remained unaccounted for by a select few individuals in this world; select few in the sense that this world was currently being ruled by the one percent that had made the headlines recently and perhaps even the individuals who were at the top of this one percent? They were the target, they were the goal, they were the new lambs to be sacrificed. After all, according to my vision, sacrifice went both ways. And it was more than time to account for all of the horrific things that had transpired within this world for the past thirty years, or so, not to mention beyond. Just far enough back in time to encompass those living souls who were truly responsible for all of the death and destruction that had occurred, and at the expense of innocent people; people who literally had no voice in their heinous destiny, who had no choice but to live at the hands of such butcherly leaders as this world had offered up.

But I truly couldn't account for the source of this wildly precarious vision; precarious because I had since learned through my own "dark night of the soul" that God loves everyone in this world. And He forgives all people as well. So what about our leaders, what about their questionable acts, what about their decisions in life that had only accumulated the hatred of the masses? Maybe our current leaders were actually right about their decisions, acts and leadership in this life. Maybe without them we would all be like a ship in the night with no predetermined course which was doomed to sink. Perhaps we really needed our world's current leadership. Even though it was flawed in the eyes of the masses, maybe it was truly the only good thing going for this world. But could this really be? Could this really be, considering all of the wars, all of the famine, all of the engineered economic chaos that was engulfing our present world? Only time would be able to tell.

But as I awoke from this stupor that had birthed a vision that was so accusatory in its demeanor, as well as its intent towards our current global leadership, I also realized one very important thing. We were running out of time. We were at what most people would refer to as "one minute before midnight"; that exact time that was as cruel as the coldest winter ever, when it came to destiny itself, the destiny of our world. We were on the brink of destruction, and maybe even our current leadership had been bamboozled about this fact, to say the least. Because karma itself was about to have its way, karma itself was going to mete out its destruction upon those countries that had tortured others, that had abused their power, that had caused so much suffering. Or was it going to be some other way? Maybe this time karma would have its way on a more personal level, a level that would "level" the playing field itself. Maybe this time karma would speak for the commoner, the person who was starving, the person who was dying from an easily treatable disease, the person whose house had just been bombed by an oil company that was in bed with our current leadership. Wow…

Could this really be true, could this actually be true? Unbelievable…undeniable…at least in terms of someone like myself, a true commoner, a truly caring individual. Could this really be true for the common person as well, the person whose children were in my care, the person who knew of no way of overcoming the power that was projected upon them by those who had more power in this world, more say as to where we were headed on a global level, more say as to where we were headed individually, more say as to where we were headed with starvation, war, destruction?

I came to, feeling way too comfortable with not

only where this vision was possibly going, but also with the way in which I was currently feeling. It was if a higher power had injected into my being a new and profound sense of energy. I stood straight up and looked at the clock. I only had two minutes in which to walk down the long hallway to pick up my class of kindergarteners at the music room.

But how could this be? How could all of this be? Why was I feeling so energized at this moment after feeling so whipped, so completely wiped out before? And why had I experienced such a vision, such an experience that seemed so completely downloaded from a higher point of view that was so distant from my own current point of view? And why was I so suddenly excited to meet my class of kindergartners and move on with this day?

The answer it would seem was lost somewhere in between my dreamy vision of global karma and my responsibilities that I had towards my classroom full of the most energetic future global leaders that I had ever encountered. After all, global leaders were born anywhere and at anytime. Global leaders came in all shapes and sizes. Global leaders weren't only comprised of the most privileged, they were comprised of the most inspired, the most talented, the most righteous. At least this is what I told myself on this particular day. And this is what I decided to believe in. I actually told myself that this world deserved the best; the best leaders that were available. Because without them, this world might become far worse than it was. It might become a wall of flames so high that even God's angels would feel the heat. Or perhaps this world might become something much better, something much more conducive to every child now entering into this abyss, this hellish abyss fraught with struggles; struggles of power, struggles of greed, struggles of…demonic visions?

HIS HELP

I remember when I found God's Love, or I should say that His Love found me. He could see that my life was crumbling. It had become a shamble of what it once was. I was at once overwhelmed with my demons and the devil, as well as all of the things that this life demanded of someone who was bent on creating the best that he could, not only for himself, but for his family. It was all I could do to ready an old Victorian house that needed to be entirely rehabilitated, not unlike my soul at the time. It was also another thing to be embattled by the devil's demons that had been sent to me directly. Between the temptation, depression, hatred, sorrow, hopelessness and confusion that was bulldozing my everyday existence along with visions of terror and apocalyptic dreams, I was losing the battle that had been placed upon my front doorstep. Even though I had been putting up the best fight possible, I was quickly going down, further than I had ever known possible, further than I had ever imagined possible, further than anyone I had ever known.

In fact suicide was on my mind. Any way would be fine. A gun had crossed my mind and sleeping pills would do just fine. These things would all take me away to where I wanted to be, anywhere else than my life at the time. But I smiled away, though, at anyone I met, at anyone I knew. I joked with my friends and I laughed with the strangers that inhabited my life as a flight attendant; the thousands of people that I met in a day that helped me traverse the thousands of miles that I flew in a day. I served them all. To the strangers I gave drinks and a smile. To my friends I gave what love I had left and to people in the grocery store and laundry mat, I gave the rest of my politeness, civility and peace. But I kept nothing for myself because I had nothing left.

I couldn't tell anyone about my problems, they all would have had me committed. I couldn't explain myself to the ministers, the priests; they would have deemed me possessed. I couldn't explain my visions to the psychologists or the psychiatrists; they would have medicated me way beyond my body's ability to assimilate the chemicals and way beyond my mind's ability to understand its new cage, its new peaceful reality, its new serene form of madness. I was all alone. But then God's Love came. Then His help came. And I didn't realize at the time how He was going to help me nor how quickly His help would arrive nor how powerful His help was going to be.

She was born on the last day of March, just past midnight. I remember looking into her eyes a few moments after she had arrived. This was all I needed to know as far as where I wanted to be for the rest of my life. I would remember our eyes meeting like this on the day she was born, forever. Two and half years later her sister was born during one of the hottest days of August. Together they would be my greatest salvation, my greatest inspiration, my greatest friends ever.

I would never have to tell them what I had been through. I would never have to relate my "dark night" to them. I would never have to think of suicide again, now that they were here, guiding me in life with their love, with God's Love. I awoke every day with a smile. Sometimes it was a tired smile. Sometimes it was a weary smile. But every smile was now fueled by a new energy in my soul that kept me going, that kept me fighting the battle that was at hand, that finally helped me to triumph over the worst part of my life that I had ever lived. And in my opinion this was the worst part of any life that I had ever lived. For, my "dark night" had been something that was almost intangible, almost unintelligible, almost unbelievable. It was something that I could not fight back against. It was something that I could not hit. It was something that was ever present, but yet absent in its ability to be summarized, to be understood, to be exited from. Its power seemed to crush with its darkness. Its depression seemed to stifle any love that was left, any hope that still smoldered within my spirit. I was breathing my last breath, when I witnessed my daughter's first.

And then things seemed to change. I now had a new focus, a new reason to live. And then there were two reasons to live. My two daughters were like an army so strong that I would never be able to lose my fight. At least this is what it seemed like to me. And this was not far from the truth. As long as I kept my eye on the ball, my focus on my family and my desire in check with what was important to my daughters, I couldn't lose. Because God was on my side with this one, He was willing and able to fulfill every need in my life, as long as it was in line with His principles, with His will, with His desire to keep us whole, a family that was loyal to His Love, His vision of Life, His desire to supply us with everything that we needed.

And while our wants were sometimes to be desired, or left unfulfilled, the surprises that he had in store for us were way beyond anything that we could have ever imagined. The laughter that He provided us with was way beyond anything that I had ever experienced. The joy that was ours was directly from Him. Our life had been completed, perfected and designed by His greatest of treasures; His Joy, His Love, His Protection, His Supply, His Hope, His Mercy, and more. Sure this world provided the wants and the needs of others, and we sometimes lacked what they had, but they didn't understand what we had in our life; the power of God. And soon we were able to showcase this, not only to ourselves, but to others as well. For, we had learned how to forgive, we had learned how to love, we had learned how to help, we had learned how to thank, we had learned how to live peacefully, we had learned how to be compassionate, and we had decided to honor His way. And we discovered that we were blessed in return...and I discovered that I was blessed beyond measure.

My fight was soon over. Sure, there were the problems that arose in our life, in my life. But we knew that God would right the wrong, as long as we prayed to Him and thanked Him for His help. This sometimes meant admitting our mistakes, admitting our weaknesses and learning from them as well. But we were willing to do what it took to remain true to God and His ideals that were in play, that were the design of our family and its destiny.

But what did this mean for the rest of the world?

How would the current unraveling global situation in this world ever be turned around, not only for our family, but for the millions of other families and innocent people around the world? Who would stop the madness that comprised the wars, the greed, the starvation, the collapse of the basic fabric of our society that was now accelerating towards the final destruction of this world? And in terms of our immediate family, would God be there to help us through these times? Would God be there to help our own community that was hurtling towards despair? Would He be there for us?

I had learned from my battle with the devil, my battle with my demons, that only prayer could help, only communion with God through thanks given to Him would yield positive results. I had learned from my "dark night" that any initiative provided by me that was not in line with God's will would surely be doomed. So I seemed only to be left with the news, the news of the wars, the news of starvation, the news of our global leadership gone wrong. I was forced to watch as this final act played itself out in a withering slew of greedy decisions, armored columns and children that starved. I was forced to acknowledge that without God's help, we would soon be dead, we would soon be forgotten by time, we would soon be a footnote upon the book of eternity and all of its stories of this world's civilizations that had succumb to humanity's worst traits, fueled by poor decisions made by the decrepit leadership that so often ruled this world. So here I was with my hands tied behind my back, my will suppressed, my hope diminishing. But I had been here before and I had seen what God could do.

He had helped me beyond reason. He had helped me with His power. I had seen how His Love could transform and how His Joy could belittle even that confusion which was so devilish. So I decided to wait, and I decided to pray, and I decided to write…just in case God needed my help, the help of a soul like mine that had once been mud, but was now as powerful as prayer, as powerful as a message in a book; a book of dreams.

A HIGHER CALLING

…but then I realized that there was another destiny for me if only I would listen. There was a path laid out for me that I had never walked before. Forget about saving the world, forget about stopping the wars, forget about ending the hunger, I just couldn't do it, nobody could do it. This world had had many wars that had been fought throughout time itself and this present day and age was no different. These wars were here to stay along with the many other forms of death, devastation and destruction that this world so neatly harbored. But there were other forms of death and destruction that hid upon a more personal plane of existence whose chaos was just as evil as any brought upon a global level. And this was what I was now aiming for.

I had seen this type of destructive chaos and the

personal wreckage that it could leave behind because I, myself, had been a stop along the way for this force that could do so much damage at the level of the soul. But I had also survived the suppression, the battle, the evil, and had won a new countenance in my victory over this force that many might call the devil. His demons had subjugated me, his dreams had frightened me and the force which he had cast right into my material world, as well, was almost enough to have sunk me forever. But I had learned how to pray and I had learned how to thank God even for those things that had not yet arrived in my life; the joy, the happiness, the love, the protection from all things evil. It had taken me time, but I had learned about these things and more and I had come out from underneath the most vicious of personal attacks that I had ever experienced.

As a result of my tenacious fight that I had initially put up, I had learned that I was not going to make it, that I was not going to win my fight without the help of a higher power, God Himself. And through steady prayer and acknowledgement that I needed God in my life every moment of every day, I began to slowly come about and withdraw from my apparent loss to the devil's confusion, fear and hatred by replacing these things with God's Love, Joy and Happiness. I had been saved from the devil, himself. And no one would be able to refute this truth, this fact; at least no one who had any knowledge about the doings of the devil and God's power to save.

And so I set my sights on a higher calling, a higher mission for me to claim. I knew that I had been saved, but I wondered if there were others; other people like me who had endured, or were enduring the devil's worst nightmares, the devil's own design. And I wondered if there were others who needed more assistance, who needed more guidance, who needed more protection from the evil that was present, from the devil and his demons. I wondered if there were others who needed to be saved from the confusion and the hatred, the fear and the visions, the danger and the destruction that the devil was offering on such a personal level. I began to openly question if there were other people like myself who were searching for something else, other than the worst of human attributes, offered by the devil and his kingdom, right here in this very world. I wondered if there were other people who were barely holding on to hope, who were losing their faith by the minute, who had lost their love and who were giving up the fight, the very important fight for their soul. I wondered if there were other people out there…just…like…this.

A NEW MANTRA

"I acknowledge that I am broke, that I have no money and that I am incapable of even making ends meet. I acknowledge that this will probably not change within my lifetime, I know that this unrelenting and withering financial force that I have succumb to will simply not end during the remaining time that I have on this earth. I realize that I may have to live with a relative or a friend and that I may have to sacrifice my pride, give up any sense of individualism, because of my current financial crisis, because of events that are beyond my ability to understand. But I do understand that I have no control over anything that may have to do with money, with my ability to make ends meet. I completely understand that while I may not have what it takes to earn an average paycheck in life, I will succumb to that which is being asked of me at this time.

I will succumb to God's will. I will not ask why and I will not complain, because I have been down this road before, I have been down this road a million times before. I am the Christian that has been sacrificed before, a millennia or two before. I will not ask God for those things that are unattainable, that are impossible for Him to deliver, for not everyone is a millionaire in this life, not everyone can have their wants and desires met, not everyone will be successful, in material terms…in material terms.

So help me to understand those things that I will never accomplish in life. Help me to understand just why minimum wage is a good thing for me and why less than minimum wage is even better, at least for me. Help me to understand why material riches are just a façade, why they are just smoke, why they are just mirrors, why they are just temporal, why they are just deceptive, why they just lead us in a direction which is undesirable. So show me why living with a relative is the best option for me in life. Show me why I cannot make it on my own, show me why I must lose at everything that I do in life. Show me why losing is such a gainful existence, losing at everything, losing to everyone. Please show me why begging on a street corner is the best of options in life for me. Show me why I must live on that which is less than a dollar a day, at times.

Please don't leave me in the dark, and don't humor me as if I were just a child. Hit me hard. Show me the tough things. Show me that no matter how hard I try to get ahead in life, I am going to fail, and fail miserably. Show me that no matter what I try to do in life to help my family, I will simply fail. Show me this because it is the truth, it is what I can expect. But please don't lie to me, please don't humor me, please don't show me your actors, your actresses, your millionaires, your billionaires, please don't show me your politicians, don't show me those people who are well, who are rich. Just show me the truth, the future of my existence. Hit me hard, please hit me hard.

But above all, show me why this is. Show me why I will never attain such financial glory, such financial independence. Show me your Kingdom and all that I can expect after I leave this world, show me your riches in the afterlife, show me that if I live a strangled life in this world that my life in the next will be filled with riches beyond my wildest dreams. And please give me the power, the strength, the wisdom to show other people just why it is that I suffer, that I cry, that I wish for death itself, that I wish for no more, but yet continue to live, continue to struggle beyond that measure that has been given to us all, that has been assigned to humanity itself. Give me the will to endure on just dollars a day, so that I may provide for not just the broken soul that I have become, but for the souls that rely on me for not just money, but for inspiration, for joy, for love, for happiness, for protection; for protection from the cold, the rain, the harshest of elements and the darkest of forces.

So please show me that a card board box is better than nothing to live in. Show me that a can of beans is better than nothing to eat. Show me that the warmth of a tattered and worn coat is better than my skin alone upon the coldest, harshest winds of winter. And please give me the presence of mind to thank you, my Creator, for all that you have bestowed upon me in this lifetime. Let me thank you for all that you have ever given me, ever blessed me with. And let me thank you for all of those things still standing in my life. Though I may have stumbled hard, though I may have fallen down in life, let me thank you for allowing me to get back up, for allowing me to stand up straight, though it be with clothes that are tattered and food that is fettered. Let me thank you for allowing me to exist and show others how it is to live, how it is to survive, so that you may take me in time, so that you may allow me in time to enter into your Kingdom.

So please give me the courage and the strength to simply exist in this world. Please give me what I need in life, give me what I desire, give me that which is connected to you. Please give me what I need to drink of, to live in, and to work on, in order to complete my humble existence in this world. And above all, please have mercy upon me, please make my time go fast, make my time so short, make my very existence in this world one of mercy, one of hope, one of joy, if that is even possible. Please hear my prayers and observe my simplest of wishes, show me how to live, how to survive, how to weather even that which is inevitable; the inevitability of my failures, the inevitability of my loss, the inevitability of my desire to die, to wither away into a different existence.

So today I pray for your intervention in my life. I pray for your new direction. I know that poverty besets me, but I pray for your supply. I know that hopelessness abounds, but I pray for your new light, your new desire for me to excel in that which is needed by you. If suffering be my plight, then let me be with you, let me be protected by your mercy, by your courage to do what is right in my life. Please let me be with you, please hear these prayers.

Above all, let me accept the fate which has been bestowed upon me. Let me accept the loss that comes my way every day. Let me turn my cheek to those who would torment me, let me forgive those who have sinned against me, against you. Let me stand tall in that face of hopelessness, let me set an example for those who depend upon me, who look up to me. And though I suffer constantly, quietly, let your love flow through me, let it flow into those who depend upon me in this life, who need me to survive. Let your joy flow through my tired body, my tired mind, into those minds who need it, who depend upon my strength, the strength that you give to me in this life. And when that time comes, let me fall into your arms that are outstretched, just waiting for my arrival into your Kingdom, let me fall into that which has been prepared for me, eternally. But give me the strength to continue until this day, give me the courage that I need to help those who depend upon me in life, who would wither without me, who would die without me. Let me go on, even though I wish for death itself. Let me live, let me love, let me give of what I have in life.

And let me thank you for these things and more. Let me live this new mantra to its fullest. Let me mock the riches that abound in certain circles in this world. Let me understand my place in this world. Let me live to see another day in which those who depend upon me will exceed my wildest expectations for them in life, and let me live so that I may try to exceed your wildest expectations for me in this life."

ANOTHER PROJECT

I sat down at one of the tables that I had so often frequented in this town that I was now living in. Most people called it Warren, but I just called it home, until I would possibly have to move again. The number of reasons that had encouraged my family and me to move throughout the years had become lost in time due to the amount of time itself that it took to not only make these moves, but to live out our lives within each of our new destinations. And Warren, Rhode Island was no different. We had only been living here for about eight months when the inevitable discussion seemed to pop into our lives. This discussion usually centered about our inability to make ends meet, as well as whether or not our kids were enjoying their new school and surroundings.

But on this particular day I had checked my worries

and fears about our financial situation at the door, so as to say, and I had proceeded to my favorite coffee shop where I ordered a familiar Americano, and a sesame seed bagel. Everything seemed to add up on this day, everything was OK. In fact I couldn't really understand why the incessant worries and fears seemed to run through my mind from time to time that were about our withering financial situation as well as other worries that seemed to plague my mind. I had used my spiritual training that I had acquired while going through my "dark night" to combat these thoughts, by praying to God for more faith in His plan. In other words, I was usually able to dispel these worries through prayer and faith in God. But lately it seemed as if even my faith and prayer couldn't keep my mind off of the inevitable- we were probably looking at a move again in the near future in order to be able to survive the economic onslaught that was taking its toll, not only on us, but on our nation and world as well. All of the moves that we had made in the past were usually made in order to increase our chances of surviving our financial malaise. But they still seemed to take their toll on us, and this new possibility of another move would only increase the amount of stress that had seemed to pile upon our shoulders and occupy our minds on a daily basis.

The thought of this seemed to melt away, though, as I took my first sip of coffee, followed by a bite of one of the best bagels I had ever enjoyed. The sun shown down upon me at the table I was sitting at outside. It cast its yellow embrace upon me with a type of mellowness and bodily warmth that could probably only be compared to a very strong narcotic; perhaps like that of a drug that could erase all worries, all fears, all confusion. So I just stared ahead, into the air that comprised the space between my table and the stores that occupied the other side of the street. I just stared for what seemed to be an eternity…no worries, no fears. These were the moments that I lived for in life…no worries, no fears.

After what seemed to be an eternity, I suddenly noticed a figure that was walking on the other side of the street. He was travelling at a slower pace, walking across my field of vision. The bright sunshine that had previously left me in a very welcome and warm kind of stupor now acted as a type of shield against what I was currently trying to observe. I could not see this man very well, almost as if he was covered by a bright halo of sunshine. Very interesting, I thought to myself. Even though I could not make out this man visually, I had the distinct impression that I had seen this man before. There was a feeling in the air, almost as if I was expecting him at this table on this very day.

As I watched him transit across the street, in front of the traffic, shuffling across the pedestrian walkway, I realized that he was headed my way. When he turned towards my direction after crossing the street, he slowly walked towards me with the shuffle, or gait, of a person that has been through a time in life that not many people would understand. At least this was the impression that this man had given me, with his slow procession towards my table that I had been sitting at while enjoying the warm day and the warm caffeine.

He proceeded to move slowly past my table and then turned into the coffee shop, all the while staring down at the sidewalk. I suddenly realized that this was the same man that I had previously seen in this town. He was the same man that had offered a kind gesture to me by waving affably at me from across the street one day. He was the same man that had been standing at the street corner one day as I had driven by him in my car, headed to this same coffee shop, but on a different day. However, on this day he was dressed as if he were no longer entertaining the idea that perhaps he was a stockbroker or a captain of some industrial undertaking. The gray suit that he had once worn was replaced by a dark green sweater and gray pants. His shiny black shoes had been replaced by sneakers, the color of pavement. It wasn't his new clothes that had made it difficult for me to realize that this was the same man that I had seen from across the street a few weeks ago, rather it was his new demeanor that had really thrown me in my attempt to place him with something familiar in my mind. He was now shuffling along the sidewalk as if he had not eaten in days, or perhaps he had been feeling sick. This new demeanor stood in stark contrast to his previously carefree attitude when he had been waving at me from across the street, an attitude that almost said, "Take this world and everything in it, and put it where you want."

He no longer seemed to have the joy and carefree attitude that he had had when I had seen him in the past. But as to why I was even noticing this about someone I did not even know was way beyond my ability to understand or fathom. Once again, it was almost as if something on a higher level was directing my attention to this man. Sure, it was he who had waved at me from across the street several months ago, and it was also this man whom I had seen while driving past him as he stood on a corner. But I had not made any attempt whatsoever to embrace this man's caring attitude towards me on that first occasion when he had been waving at me, almost waving at the world, showing everyone that he was joy itself, wrapped up in a lovingly carefree style and grace.

He was only in there for a few moments, but when he exited the coffee shop, he shuffled by me and then stopped, empty handed. He continued to look down at the sidewalk as he investigated his right pocket, perhaps for some change or a misplaced dollar. He then looked around and moved over to the table that was next to mine and sat down. I couldn't help it. As he surveyed his new surroundings, I looked over at him and studied his eyes for a moment. His gaze then met mine. His green eyes pierced mine for a brief moment. We studied each other. I could tell that this man was comfortable with this type of gaze, almost as if he had been used to people staring at him throughout his years. I smiled at him and he returned my smile through his eyes that seemed to recognize a stranger who was going to be nice, who was going to be kind to him. I got up from my chair and moved over to his table. As I sat down, a brief handshake ensued.

"Hi, I'm Elijah, who are you?"

"Verily I say unto you, Except ye be converted, and become as little children, ye shall not enter into the kingdom of heaven."

-Jesus

COMING SOON-

WWW.THE444CONNECTION.COM